DATA DRIVEN

DATA DRIVEN

SOLVING THE BIGGEST PROBLEMS IN STARTUP INVESTING

AMAL BHATNAGAR

NEW DEGREE PRESS

COPYRIGHT © 2021 AMAL BHATNAGAR

DATA DRIVEN

Solving the Biggest Problems in Startup Investing

ISBN   978-1-63730-643-7   *Paperback*
           978-1-63730-726-7   *Kindle Ebook*
           978-1-63730-917-9   *Ebook*

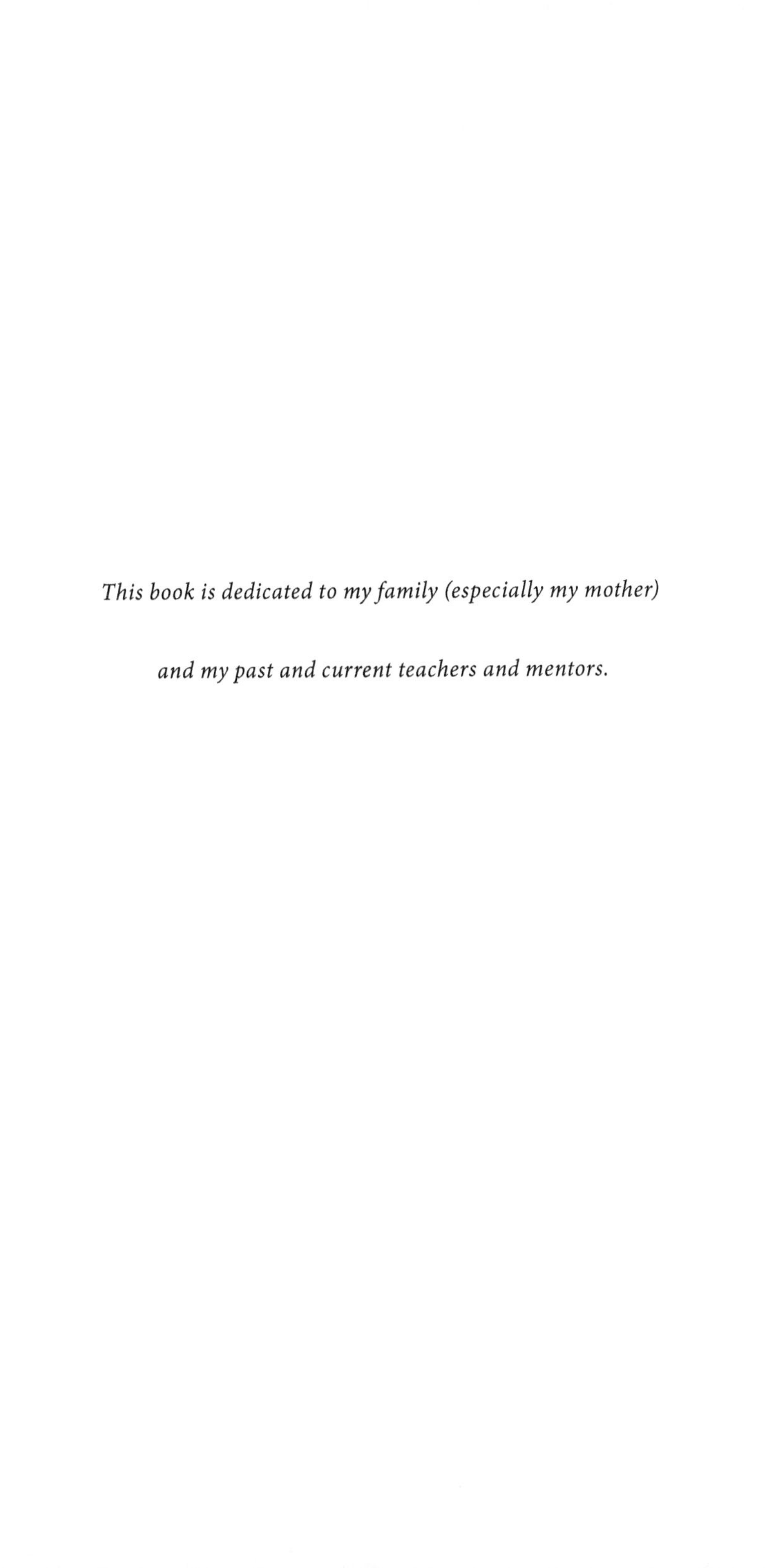

This book is dedicated to my family (especially my mother)

and my past and current teachers and mentors.

Contents

INTRODUCTION 9

PART 1.   **FUNDAMENTALS OF VENTURE CAPITAL**   **13**

CHAPTER 1.   VENTURE CAPITAL 101. 15

CHAPTER 2.   HOW VENTURE CAPITALISTS SPEND
THEIR TIME 21

CHAPTER 3.   OUR DATA IS BROKEN 33

CHAPTER 4.   FUNDRAISING IS HARD 45

PART 2.   **THE JOURNEY TO BECOMING DATA-DRIVEN**   **57**

CHAPTER 5.   DECIDE TO BECOME DATA-DRIVEN 59

CHAPTER 6.   BUILD YOUR OWN DATA 65

CHAPTER 7.   LEVERAGE CROWDSOURCED DATA 75

CHAPTER 8.   CREATE YOUR DATA TEAM 83

PART 3.   **DATA-DRIVEN INVESTING TECHNIQUES**   **95**

CHAPTER 9.   REMOVE BIAS 97

CHAPTER 10. PARTNER WITH TOP CO-INVESTORS 107

CHAPTER 11. PREDICT STARTUP SUCCESS 119

CHAPTER 12. MEASURE COMPANY TRACTION 131

CHAPTER 13. BUILD TOOLS WITH EMAIL DATA 141

CHAPTER 14. ARM RETAIL INVESTORS WITH DATA 149

CHAPTER 15. THE ULTIMATE DATA-DRIVEN INVESTOR . . 159

ACKNOWLEDGMENTS 163

APPENDIX 167

Introduction

I am a data scientist/data product manager at a hypergrowth, California-based, fintech startup. As the company's first data hire, I build data products and further establish the company as a data leader in the industry. I completed my undergraduate degree from the University of California at Berkeley, earning a dual degree in data science and economics. Given that UC Berkeley is in the Bay Area, many venture capital (VC) investors held guest lectures, coffee chats, and one-on-one sessions with students. Learning how VCs help startups grow, build innovative solutions, and change the world made VC appealing to me.

My undergraduate coursework allowed me to take a full spectrum of classes across various departments, such as computer science, statistics, economics, and mathematics. During the day, I learned about complex technical topics, such as building incredibly accurate neural network algorithms and complicated statistical distributions. During the night, I worked on side hustles, such as founding my own startups, writing for the *Times of India*, and developing my own data software. By working on various projects, I met ambitious student founders, amazing faculty, and futuristic investors.

Over time, I started to identify overlap between my education and side projects. I noticed many opportunities to apply the concepts I learned in my classes toward my projects. Soon enough, I discovered the niche intersection between venture capital and data science. Intrigued to learn more, I began researching how VCs use data science. Unfortunately, I could not find many articles, tutorials, or online resources that comprehensively explained how VCs leverage data science to invest in startups.

The more data scientists, founders, and VCs I talked to, the more I realized how big of a problem not having centralized data-led resources was. **The newer VCs I spoke to wanted to be data-driven, but they just did not know where to start.**

Motivated to help new VCs, I began to aggregate my research and write this book. Although I encourage everyone to read this book, it will be most helpful to:

- New VCs who want to adopt data-driven techniques;
- Existing VCs who want to become more data-driven; and
- Data scientists who want to apply their skills in the inter-section of investing and entrepreneurship.

My goal for this book is to show:

- Strategies that leadership and data teams can implement to build data-driven firms;

- Potential data sources and techniques for data teams to explore and aggregate novel and proprietary datasets; and
- Lessons from data-driven investors who previously leveraged data to solve some of VC's most pressing issues.

When writing this book, I spoke with some of the brightest minds in the industry. They provided valuable feedback and insights on how they built data-driven firms. I broke the book down into three parts:

- Part One—Introduces the VC world and its three biggest problems
- Part Two—Isolates the steps that new data-driven VCs must take
- Part Three—Narrates how data-driven investors built their data products from scratch

If you are already familiar with VC, I suggest you go directly to parts two and three. If you are new to the startup space, I recommend reading all three parts.

I define a data-driven investor as one who:

- Runs experiments to test hypotheses
- Makes objective decisions based on data
- Actively collects proprietary data and public data
- Builds data products to solve problems

With that said, let's explore how we can become **data-driven investors** and solve some of startup investing's biggest problems.

1

FUNDAMENTALS OF VENTURE CAPITAL

Venture Capital 101

When you were a kid, you might have started a lemonade stand on your front lawn.

I sure did.

I remember dashing to the nearby grocery store with my parents, running to the produce aisle, and inspecting all the lemons to find the smoothest, brightest, and heaviest ones.

I remember scouring through the garage for banners, writing phrases such as "Fresh Lemonade" and "World's Best Lemonade," and planting the homemade signs throughout the neighborhood.

I remember sitting at my stand, battling the scorching heat, and selling my freshly made lemonade to friends and neighbors.

Most of all, I remember taking all the money from our homemade cash register, which was just a Ziploc bag, stacking the quarters and dollars on top of each other, and feeling my smile grow every time I saw the day's total revenue.

My parents let me keep all the profit and asked for nothing in return.

Suppose they did, though. Suppose we agreed that for every dollar of profit I make, I gave my parents fifty cents back. In other words, we would share the profits fifty-fifty, in which they would invest money, and I would manage and operate the business. They would be the startup's investors, and I would be its founder.

Venture capital (VC) works similarly.

WHAT IS VENTURE CAPITAL?

Suppose I want to go back to selling lemonade like when I was a kid, but now I want to sell nationally or globally. I would need to hire a sales team to find retail stores to sell the lemonade at, sign agreements with manufacturing plants to produce my lemonade at scale, and invest in research and development to discover ways to make healthier and tastier lemonade than my competitors.

This plan requires a considerable amount of capital. VCs can fund my business if I prove two pillars:

- **Increasing product traction**—Customers need to buy my lemonade. My startup needs to grow in as many ways as possible. For example, the number of stores that sell our product, the number of new and returning customers, and the total business revenue should all increase monthly.

- **Exit strategy**—I need to strategize my startup's exit plan. VCs will make money if another company acquires my startup or my company becomes large enough to have an initial public offering, or an IPO. They won't invest in my company if I do not demonstrate how and why we may have an exit.

> *Initial Public Offering (IPO)—According to Investopedia, private companies offer to sell their shares to the public. Anyone who owned the stocks before the IPO, such as founders, investors, and employees, can buy shares before the IPO at cheaper prices and sell them at IPO to realize their gains.*

> *Exit—Strategic plan to liquidate shares of the company through an acquisition or IPO (Investopedia 2021).*

According to Nicole Gravagna and Peter K. Adams's book, *Venture Capital for Dummies*, venture capitalists only make money in three ways:

1. Management fee
2. Carried interest upon an exit
3. Carried interest from employees' own investments

Management fee—Large institutions, such as pension funds, university endowments, and insurance companies, give

VCs money, usually millions of dollars, to invest in startups. These large institutions are called limited partners, or LPs. The VCs allocate a small percent, usually 2 percent, of the total amount given by LPs as management fees to pay for its operations. This funds employee salaries, legal fees, and office rental space. The VCs invest the remaining 98 percent in startups. For example, several LPs might collectively give a VC one hundred million dollars. The VC will then spend two million dollars on funding its operations.

```
2% Management Fees on $100M Fund = $2M
```

Carried interest upon an exit—VCs make money when a company it invested in exits. The VCs usually keep 20 percent of the net profit, which is the difference between the fund's initial capital and the fund's final return. For example, a venture firm could have invested one hundred million dollars across several startups. Over a few years, some exit while others fail, and the VC fund makes $150 million. It will return the initial capital invested and 80 percent of the net profit to its LPs. It keeps the remaining 20 percent as its revenue, also known as "carry."

```
Amount Returned to LPs = $100M + (80% *
          ($150M - $100M)) = $140M
```

```
VC Carry = 20% * ($150M - $100M) = $10M
```

Carried interest from employees' own investments—
When some VCs decide to partner with startups, they may allow their employees to also invest with their own money. Employees may do so if they personally believe the startup will be successful.

> *Limited partner (LP)—Institutional investors who give VCs money to partner with startups. They rarely directly interact with the VC's daily operations (Investopedia 2021).*

VCs need to generate returns worth around three times their investments. Otherwise, their LPs may decide to invest elsewhere, such as real estate funds, private equity funds, or publicly traded stocks. The S&P 500, which is the investing benchmark for the public markets, started in 1926. According to the finance platform Investopedia, since then and 2018, it achieved an annualized return of almost 11 percent. VCs need to attain at least an 11 percent annualized return for LPs to invest their money in venture capital instead of the S&P 500.

For example, if an LP is deciding its investment strategy for the next ten years, it can either choose to invest in either the stock market or venture capital. If they invest in the stock market, they can expect a 2.84-times return. If they invest in a ten-year VC fund, they should earn more than that to warrant its illiquidity and risk. That means if a venture firm wants to create a ten-year fund, then it needs to return at least three times the initial investment.

Expected Ten-Year Return for the S&P 500:
$$(1.11)^{10} = 2.84$$

- 1.11 represents the 11 percent annual return
- 10 is how long the fund will run for
- 2.84 is the total return

A VC that raised one hundred million dollars from LPs should invest in strong startups so they can return **at least** $284 million.

KEY LESSONS TO BECOMING DATA-DRIVEN

- Quantify the target return based on current stock market conditions.
- Strategize your startup portfolio construction. Either you can invest in a few startups you strongly believe will exit or invest in many startups that you moderately believe will exit.

CHAPTER 2

How Venture Capitalists Spend Their Time

To generate a three-times return, venture capitalists need to invest in startups they truly believe will succeed. They need to look at many opportunities before deciding which ones to partner with. This means VCs need to spend their time as efficiently as possible.

This book aims at demonstrating how investors can leverage data to be more efficient. Before exploring potential solutions, we must first understand how VCs currently spend their time.

In 2013, Hunter Walk, a Stanford University Graduate School of Business alum who led consumer products at Google, co-founded the venture firm Homebrew Capital with Satya Patel, a former vice president at Twitter and former partner at Battery Ventures. The two worked together to invest in leading technology startups, such as Plaid and Cruise. Soon after co-founding the investing firm, Walk wrote a blog post titled *How VCs Spend Their Time. Err, How This VC Spends*

His Time. In it, he walks through their responsibilities. As shown in the graph below, they spend half their time evaluating investment opportunities and a third of their time supporting portfolio companies. They split the remaining time in building relationships and managing the fund operations. This time distribution indicates they consider evaluating startup opportunities their most important responsibility.

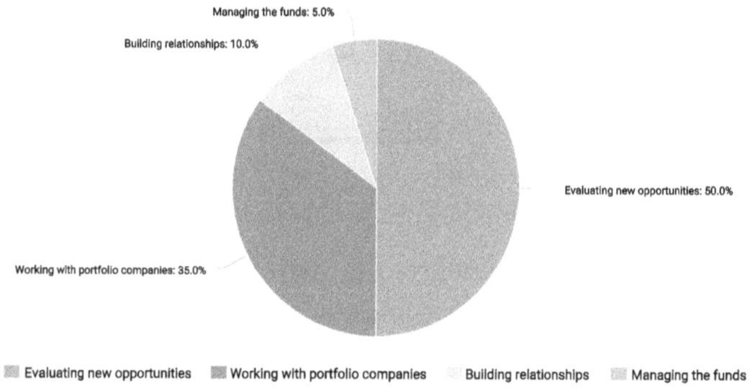

Figure 1: How Homebrew Capital Spends Its Time

EVALUATE NEW STARTUP PARTNERSHIP OPPORTUNITIES

Homebrew Capital is a seed-stage venture firm. Startups at the seed-stage often only have a minimum viable product (MVP), which is a product prototype that helps founders gather customer feedback and a few users. Because the startups are so new, they may show limited historical traction. Seed-stage startups often have many years remaining in their journey until they reach an exit. Sammy Abdullah from Crunchbase, a well-known data platform within the VC community, investigated 127 publicly traded technology company's S-1 files, which are documents that companies must fill out upon an IPO, and found that software-as-a-service companies spend a median of nine years to IPO, while business-to-consumer companies take a median of seven years. This means when seed-stage founders and investors decide to partner, they plan to collaborate for potentially up to a decade.

The limited data points and long timeframe for an exit means seed-stage investors must bet on the founders more than just the MVP. Investors look for entrepreneurs who are resilient enough to conquer difficult obstacles in the future, flexible enough to pivot the company based on customer feedback and market trends, and experienced enough to know which problems to prioritize. On the other side of the table, early-stage founders look for strategic investors who can provide both the capital and resources to build and scale their companies. Founders may seek VCs who can introduce them to other investors, tap into a large network of professionals to onboard talent, and leverage their prior experiences to advise them through impossible decisions.

Finding the right entrepreneurs to partner with can be broken down into two steps:

1. Finding each other
2. Evaluating founder-investor fit

The first step requires its own battle. Many early-stage founders I know take between six and nine months to find the investors they eventually partner with.

The second step depends more on chemistry and trust. Founders and investors must interact with each other long enough to know if they are the right fit for each other. In 2020, a seed-stage investor told me he meets with founders between fifteen and twenty times to evaluate the fit.

If the investors already know the founders, the second step takes far less time. In the same blog post as before, Walk explained he and Patel previously spent less than a day to invest in a startup if they already knew the startup's founding team. On the other hand, if Walk or Patel did not previously know the team, then they may take longer to invest. Walk wrote, "When we didn't know the founders already, [the] **fastest** we've gotten from [first meeting the founders to writing an investment check] is ten days."

Knowing the founders ahead of time helps. The graph below shows how much quicker Walk and Patel have taken to invest in founders they previously knew versus those they did not previously know.

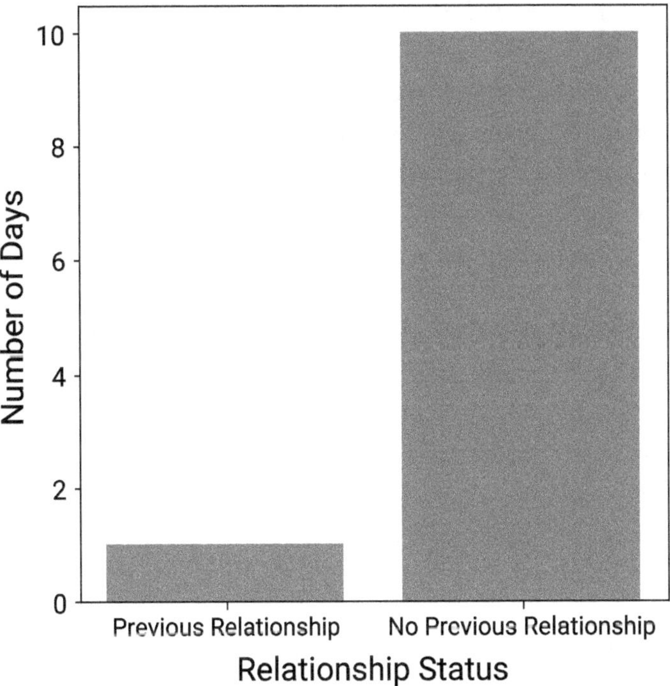

Figure 2: Fastest Deals Signed between Previously Known and Unknown Founders

Prior relationships help but do not guarantee investments. The venture firm still must research the startup and industry to decide whether to offer an investment. This step is called "due diligence." In the same blog, Homebrew Capital isolated its three steps of due diligence.

> **Due diligence**—*According to Investopedia, investors thoroughly investigate the startup by reviewing historical financials, company documents, and*

other relevant files that represent the startup's traction and future potential.

First, Walk or Patel meet with the founders to learn more about the startup. By the end of the meeting, they hypothesize why the startup will be successful. If they can envision a world where the startup solves the intended problems, then they will meet with the founders again.

Second, Walk and Patel both do deeper due diligence on the startup. They research the industry, use the product themselves, and talk to the startup's customers. When they do meet with the founders again, they ask more detailed questions about the company's strategy and may request specific data points that represent the product's traction, such as financials and references.

Finally, if they have full confidence in the founders and the startup's exit strategy, Walk and Patel may offer to invest. They outline their investment terms and encourage the founders to evaluate them as partners. Walk and Patel provide a reference sheet with people, whether it be other investors or entrepreneurs of companies the two invested in who can tell the founders what it's like to work with Homebrew Capital. This helps the entrepreneurs evaluate the founder-investor fit.

Due diligence takes time. Both parties need to meticulously assess if they are right for each other before deciding to partner.

SUPPORT PORTFOLIO COMPANIES

Once a VC invests in a startup, it cannot just write a check and walk away. Rather, the investors proactively help their portfolio companies succeed—it's part of the job description!

Walk and Patel actively coordinate with the founders of their portfolio companies, which are the startups the VC previously invested in, to identify their biggest problems and strategize potential solutions. For example, if the startup tells them its biggest challenge is not signing enough new customers, then the two investors may thoroughly search their network to see who previously onboarded new customers in their own organizations and may decide to connect them with the founders. Scheduling frequent meetings with the founders helps the investors know how they can help and fix problems.

> **Portfolio company**—*According to Investopedia, a portfolio is a collection of the investments a VC has made. Each company in the portfolio is referred to as a portfolio company.*

The best investors do everything they can to help their companies. Many investors have either previously worked in hypergrowth startups or built a startup themselves. They have seen firsthand how hard it is to create a successful company. Before founding Homebrew Capital, the co-founders worked in scaling technology companies. Seeing how difficult it can be to grow a company taught them the humility they now use with portfolio companies. Walk wrote that their previous backgrounds "[gave them] insight and empathy into the founder journey." The investors take it upon themselves to schedule frequent lunches, one-on-ones, and board meetings to discuss pressing problems and strategize solutions.

DEVELOP NEW RELATIONSHIPS

Venture capital is a human-centric profession. Entrepreneurs want to work with investors who have strong reputations for humility, understanding, and empathy. Venture investors build brands that highlight their values. Having a positive brand simplifies the process of finding other investors to work with and meeting high-quality startups.

For example, if a startup wants to raise ten million dollars, it doesn't turn to just one investor. Several VCs contribute to meet the required amount. One VC usually takes the lead and invests the most. For example, four VCs can invest in a startup, in which three invest two million dollars each and one invests four million dollars. The VC that invested four million dollars becomes the "lead investor." Having a track record of investing in successful startups encourages the co-investors to partner with the lead investor.

Entrepreneurs look for investors with strong, positive reputations too. When fundraising, founders often ask each other who they should potentially partner with. An investor with a bad reputation would not get many referrals. But if an investor is known to be an industry expert, help founders during difficult times, and have the startups' best interests at heart, then that investor will get many referrals from founders.

To build Homebrew Capital's brand, Walk frequently speaks with new founders and advises them regardless of whether he invests. He also shares his investing experiences on social media and speaks at conferences.

MANAGE FUND LOGISTICS

VCs cannot operate without initial capital.

As previously mentioned, venture investors raise capital from limited partners. Although they do invest with some of their own money, venture investors mostly invest with the LPs' money. To raise capital from limited partners in the future, venture investors need to analyze their current investments' performance, prepare legal documents, and strategize on market trends. They need to explain how they are using their current LPs' money and why future LPs should invest in them.

Venture capitalists also need to grow their own team. They spend time hiring investment associates, vice presidents, and partners to source more startup opportunities and better support current portfolio companies. Many large and established venture capitalists built their own software to manage operations and find potential deals, so they may hire for their technology teams to keep their software updated.

OTHER VCS MANAGE TIME SIMILARLY

Spending a lot of time in due diligence—or as Walk described as "evaluating new opportunities"—is not uncommon.

David Hornik from August Capital, a venture firm with more than $2.5 billion under assets according to its website, spends similar amounts of time when determining which companies to invest in. In 2016, he gave a guest lecture at Columbia University, where he explained that he spends 250 hours looking at more than one thousand companies annually. Hornik broke down the numbers:

1. He looks at more than one thousand startup executive summaries.
2. He schedules a one-hour meeting with one hundred startups. He determines whether to meet with the startup based on the referral and product vision.
3. He then meets with ten of the one hundred startups for about ten hours each. During this phase, he tracks metrics, asks more detailed questions, and better understands the entrepreneurs.
4. He invests in one or two startups.

Out of the one thousand-plus startups he could invest in, he only partners with one or two annually. That's an investment rate of 0.2 percent! According to his firm's website, some of his successful investments that had IPOs are Splunk, GitLab, and Fastly.

Other venture investors spend their time like Homebrew Capital. In 2016, the *Twenty Minute VC*, which is the largest independent venture capital podcast with more than 100,000 listeners, brought Manu Kumar, the Founder of K9 Ventures, on as a guest speaker. Explained in a *TechCrunch* article, Kumar surveyed one hundred venture capital firms to understand better how they spend their time. He found, as shown in the graph below, that VCs spend a third of their time determining which startups to invest in. They spend about the same amount of time supporting their portfolio companies. VCs specifically said they wish they spent more than 31 percent of their time on relationship building and fund logistics.

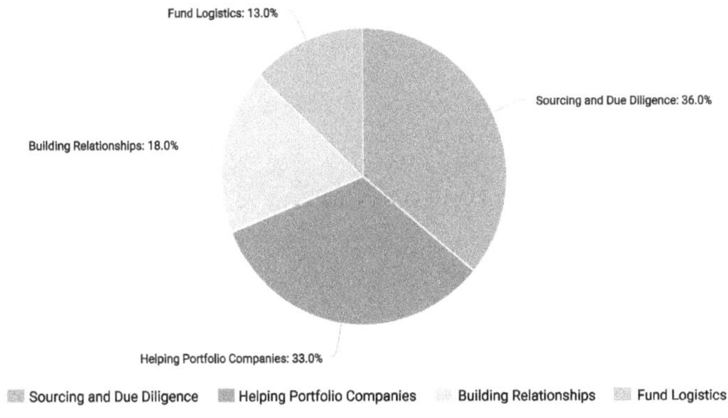

Figure 3: Kumar's Survey Findings on How VCs Spend Time

KEY LESSONS TO BECOMING DATA-DRIVEN

- Investors spend most of their time looking at which start-ups to invest in. This is their biggest priority and our biggest opportunity to automate.
- VCs want to spend more time on other responsibilities but can't.
- VC is a human-centric profession that requires understanding the founders' personalities and values.

CHAPTER 3

Our Data Is Broken

When I ask venture capitalists about the most difficult part about their job, they most commonly cite the industry's limited available data.

They retort that data opaqueness makes it difficult to know which startups to invest in. Many find it more challenging to invest in the private markets—investments that are only available to institutional investors—than in the public markets—investments that are open to everyone. Stock market investors can gather a plethora of data on publicly traded companies, but venture capitalists scramble to find a fraction of information on startups.

Most VCs I've talked to—both data-driven and non-data-driven—agree that predictive analytics and data-led investing may play a large role in the future. The most immediate problem, though, is that **new VCs do not have enough existing data to work with**, especially compared to the incumbent VCs who have operated for decades and stored unparalleled amounts of data. FundComb, a platform that helps match founders with investors, aggregated a list of the oldest VC firms.

Table 1: Oldest Venture Capital Firms

Venture Capital Firm	**Age (As of 2021)**
Bessemer Venture Partners	110 years old
Norwest Venture Partners	60 years old
Greylock Partners	56 years old
Venrock	52 years old
Kleiner Perkins	49 years old

The disproportional amount of data that a hundred-year-old firm and a brand-new firm may have epitomizes the problem of asymmetric data. **Large, incumbent VCs can leverage their deep data to ascertain whether to invest in a startup, while new VCs most likely cannot.**

New investors may be tempted to quickly create a large dataset from public sources and level up with incumbent VCs. However, new investors should not rashly exclusively use publicly available data without understanding its potential consequences. Although commercially available data can help the investors step in the right direction, the data can be flawed, skewing the validity of any analysis. For example, Politecnico di Torino's Giuseppe Carlo Calafiore and his research team knew that investing in startups is risky. The team decided to help investors by building a machine learning model to predict the likelihood that a startup will be successful in the future—a problem that almost every VC would like to solve.

According to their paper titled *A Classifiers Voting Model for Exit Prediction of Privately Held Companies,* they used the data from Thomson Reuters Eikin, a platform that contains financial information on 83,544 companies across nine industries dated between 1996 and 2018. The dataset included each startup's investors, fundraising data, formation data, and outcome. The research team could use those columns to determine a startup's success based on its fundraising frequency, most recent fundraise, and prior investors. Unfortunately, the data had its flaws. After learning that the data since 2012 was too incomplete to use, Giuseppe Carlo Calafiore's research group decided to only look at the data between 1995 and 2011. Removing seven years' worth of information reduced the dataset down to 55,000 companies, which is 34 percent smaller than the original dataset. They tested many different machine learning models.

Eventually, the team developed a model that correctly predicted whether a startup would succeed or fail 63 percent of the time!

Giuseppe Carlo Calafiore's research group showed that machine learning could technically be used to predict startup success. **The model could have been more accurate** if they did not have to remove the ~30,000 incomplete observations. If those data points were usable, then the model would have had more information to train on and learn from. Additionally, removing the data from 2012 onward makes the model mostly applicable to startups before 2012 and less useful for predicting startup activity a decade later. Machine learning algorithms work well on the data it is trained on. If it is used on new, unseen data that is drastically different from the training data, then the model may perform poorly. This phenomenon is known as overfitting.

Giuseppe Carlo Calafiore's attempt at modeling startup success highlights the importance of collecting accurate data. If new VCs **only** use publicly available or commercial data, then they risk the biases, exaggerations, and inconsistencies that come with them.

ANALYZING PUBLIC COMPANIES IS NOT ENOUGH

When new VCs first start to compile a dataset, they can and should incorporate data on publicly traded companies. As stated on the website of the US Securities and Exchange Commission, also known as the SEC, when startups decide to IPO, the SEC requires them to file certain documents, such as an IPO prospectus and S-1 registrations. They both disclose previously private information, such as key stakeholders, future plans, and potential risks. Since every publicly traded company must disclose this information, the documents can be a gold mine of data.

No matter how tempting the SEC data might seem, VCs must supplement it with additional data on failed startups. Excluding data on companies that wanted to IPO but could not leads to survivorship bias (Culture Amp 2017). The data provided by the SEC only represents successful companies and does not include the companies that did not have an IPO, ergo startups that investors might consider as failed startups. If VCs apply learnings from SEC data onto all startups, then they are excluding patterns from failed startups. For example, if new VCs go through the data on recent IPO companies and find that 90 percent of the CEOs went to Ivy League schools, then VCs may conclude that an Ivy League education can predict startup success. What they fail to consider is that there may be many startups with Ivy League-educated CEOs, but the startups still failed. Just because some successful startups have Ivy League-educated CEOs does not mean that failed startups do not have Ivy League-educated CEOs. If VCs only invest in Ivy League-led startups, then they will inevitably invest in startups that may fail.

> *Survivorship Bias—The fallacy that successful investments represent all investments, including the ones that failed (Investopedia 2021).*

The disproportionately unequal number of public and private companies exacerbates the survivorship bias. The University of Chicago's Steven Kaplan and Harvard Business School's Josh Lerner wrote a paper together titled *Venture Capital Data: Opportunities and Challenges,* where they found that "only a relatively model fraction of venture-backed companies go public." In 2020, 494 companies had an IPO, according to FactSet. If new VCs only look at the SEC documents for companies that recently IPO'd, then they would only know the background of the ~500 companies that IPO'd, not the thousands that are still private. Applying the trends from recently IPO'd companies onto actively private or previously failed companies is illogical at best and unethical at worst.

Tracking data on both successful and failed startups helps mitigate survivorship bias.

The good news is that there have been previous attempts to track all startups and compile this information into commercially available databases.

The bad news is that many of these attempts failed.

PREVIOUS ATTEMPTS AT TRACKING ALL STARTUPS FAILED

To compensate for the lack of data on startup performance, several private companies have set out to create their own databases. In the same paper by Kaplan and Lerner mentioned earlier, the authors explained that the two most used databases were Thomson Reuters' *VentureXpert* (VX) and the Dow Jones' *Venture Source* (VS). The former had data since 1961, while the latter had data since 1994. The two authors claim both platforms did a great initial job in centralizing startup data, but over time, they started to show problems. It is hard for new VCs to use the databases if they do not correct for the data's inherent biases.

INCONSISTENT AND INFLATED STARTUP DATA

New VCs need to make sure any datasets they use are accurate and representative of the current startup scene. If the underlying data is flawed, then any consequential analysis may be flawed too.

According to Kaplan and Lerner, a research group out of the University of California at Davis measured the quality of the data found in the VX and VS databases. They examined how the VS and VX data on forty investments between 1993 and

2003 compared against those companies' actual outcomes. The team aggregated accurate data on the forty investments from external sources to compare against the data found in the VX and VS datasets.

They found the data from VX and VS were out of date. First, both databases underestimated the number of companies that have shut down. VX reported that 10 percent of the companies had shut down when the research group found that 20 percent of the companies did. Second, VX stopped reporting companies' exits as much. They believe that this signals "a lack of investment in collecting new data." Although the two databases started to aggregate and display information, their accuracy decreased over time.

Kaplan and Lerner also believe the databases tend to show inflated startup valuations for early-stage startups. In their paper, they specifically wrote that "less established groups, or those seeking to raise new funds in the near future, may be tempted to shade these valuations upward." Traditionally, startups are valued based on financial metrics, such as the price-to-earnings ratio and discounted cash flow, to reflect the company's financial health. Because many early-stage startups have limited revenue, VCs understandably cannot accurately predict future revenue. As early-stage startups mature, their revenue tends to look like a hockey stick. The first few months of revenue are flat, and then once the startup starts to gain significant traction and find product-market fit, then the revenue increases exponentially.

To make up for the lack of revenue, Kaplan and Lerner write that-early-stage VCs may replace financial metrics with intangible ones. Investors resort to using "complex, frequently subjective assessments of a venture's technology, expected market opportunity, and its management team's prowess" to justify their portfolio companies' valuations. One person can find the startup's technology incredibly valuable, while the next person may not. The databases cannot adjust the valuation data that VCs provide them. As a result, the two co-authors find that "these inflated valuations may find their way into databases." The databases are not at fault. Rather, the problem is that deciding how much early-stage startups should be worth is difficult in general. New VCs just need to be cautious that valuations may be inflated.

We can more clearly understand how big of a problem this is by comparing it to sports. Suppose you are playing basketball with your friends at your local park. You previously played with your friends, but you don't remember how impactful everyone was. You do remember some ad hoc stats, like the number of points some players scored and the number of rebounds other players made. When you are picking teams, your friends hype themselves up. They exclaim:

- "Pick me! I know you and I can play well together."
- "I didn't play well last game because I never got the ball."
- "I've been working on my dribbling skills. No one has seen them yet."

Because you don't remember how well each person played, you don't have a consistent mental database. As a result, you must choose your team based on what the players tell you, not on what you have seen!

Likewise, due to inconsistent and inflated data, VCs decide which companies to partner with based on qualitative factors. VCs are not at fault. They are put in a difficult position to make investment decisions based on subjective factors.

INABILITY TO ANALYZE OTHER VCS

It is human behavior for new VCs to investigate which startups their fellow VCs are investing in. Unfortunately, commercial data may not always accurately reflect other VCs' investment activity.

In the paper previously cited, Kaplan and Lerner explain that the Investment Company Act of 1940 may be responsible for the lack of clear data. Congress and President Franklin D. Roosevelt passed legislation after the Great Recession to hold institutional investors accountable and be transparent. It required public investment companies to openly disclose information and file documents with the government, helping retail investors. For example, the Investment Company Act of 1940 protects retirement accounts, because mutual funds provide these accounts, and the legislation mandates transparency from mutual funds. However, the law does not apply to venture capital. VC firms are not held to the same standard of disclosure and transparency.

Additionally, databases don't frequently track first-time funds. Kaplan and Lerner found that, as stated in their research paper, "Many first-time funds do not have any institutional investors and may not be captured by commercial data providers unless they successfully raise a second fund." This causes a backfill bias. Databases only show data on the VCs that invested successfully in their first fund and raised future funds. They exclude data on the VCs that only raised one fund. This makes it difficult for first-time VCs to see how **all** other first-time funds usually perform.

WE CANNOT EASILY COMBINE DIFFERENT DATABASES

When I first learned about each of the problems mentioned above, I asked myself, "Why can't we just combine all the databases? If some databases have some information, and other databases have other information, then if we combine them, we should have a complete dataset!"

Unfortunately, it isn't that easy.

Each database tends to define its terms differently.

For example, Kaplan and Lerner found that several databases define a fund's start date differently:

- Burgiss defines it as the year the fund first gets money from LPs.
- Cambridge Associates defines it as the year the fund was first legally formed.
- Preqin defines it as the year the venture firm invests in its first startup using the capital from the fund.

New VCs may want to know if other VCs' funds are still active. VCs tend to actively invest in startups during the first three to five years of their fund length. A new VC may want to refer to the databases and find other active VC firms to co-invest with on future deals. There is no guarantee that all three of these events—the fund legally forming, raising capital from LPs, and investing in its first company—happen all in the same year. If a fund legally formed in 2014 but didn't invest in a startup until 2015, then the databases would show different years.

Datasets may also define the types of investors differently. Angel investors and VCs tend to partner with early-stage startups and buyout funds, and private equity firms invest in later-stage startups. However, according to Kaplan and Lerner, each database categorizes the types of investors differently. For example, a VC who invests in all types of companies, ranging from early-stage to late-stage, might be labeled as a venture capital firm in one database but as a private equity or buyout fund in another database. If a VC firm is misclassified as a private equity firm in a database, then angel investors or venture capitalists that use the database will most likely not reach out to the misclassified firm.

Each database follows a different set of logic when defining their features. If VCs want to combine each database to create a comprehensive internal dataset, then they need to account for the potential differences in definitions prior to merging them. Otherwise, they risk creating an inconsistent and inaccurate dataset.

When I exchanged emails with Kaplan, he told me that current database companies, such as PitchBook, are working on solving these data gaps. As a Board Member of PitchBook's parent company called MorningStar, he knows firsthand the problems that data platforms face. Future data companies and VCs should listen to his advice and learnings.

Creating the commercial databases mentioned above must have required a large amount of work. Keeping them updated is very challenging. Thanks to the teams that developed the commercial databases, we have a great foundation of data we wouldn't have otherwise. As more and more VCs become data-driven, we can work together to update the commercial databases. This book's goal is to help the investing industry move forward, and the commercial databases help us create the necessary groundwork to do so.

Despite the databases' flaws, VCs shouldn't ignore them. Rather, they can find ways to mitigate the bias and supplement them with the new, internal data they track themselves.

KEY LESSONS TO BECOMING DATA-DRIVEN
- Large, incumbent firms have operated for decades. New VCs may need to collect as much data as they can quickly and responsibly.
- Having higher-quality data leads to impactful business use cases, such as predicting startup success.
- Do not exclusively use data on public companies. Complement it with data on actively private or previously failed companies.
- Existing commercially available data may be inconsistent, biased, and flawed.
- When you create your dataset, invest resources in maintaining them for consistency and define the columns so they can be merged with other external data sources easily.

CHAPTER 4

Fundraising Is Hard

Data-driven investors should make decisions based on data. If VCs track and examine fundraising-related data, then they may notice that fundraising is difficult for all types of founders, but it is more difficult for certain groups than for others.

THE HARSH REALITIES OF FOUNDERS' LIVES

Seed-stage venture capital is hard. By the time first-time seed-stage founders begin their next round of fundraising, they have already spent months or years building the foundations of their businesses. They developed and tested their minimal viable product, built a team, and found some degree of product-market fit. To help their startup scale to the next level of success, seed-stage founders may look for Series A funding.

The entrepreneurs first set out to find the investors who would be the best fit for them. The founders go online, search for firms they think would be most relevant, and scour websites for any contact information.

They face their first roadblock. Many investment firms don't publicize their email addresses.

No problem. Founders are resilient. They get creative and search the firms' previous blog publications, investors' LinkedIn pages, and third-party email fetching services for contact information.

They finally find the email address. Quickly, they send the investors their pitch and take a sigh of relief.

A few days go by, and the entrepreneurs have not yet received a response. They decide to follow up.

Another few days go by—still, no response.

Confusion and worry start to grow. They send the investors a LinkedIn message in hopes of hearing back.

Some investors eventually respond. Most don't.

First-time founders who do not yet know many venture capitalists constantly face this frustrating and disheartening experience. I have spoken to many types of first-time founders—both student founders and industry veterans.

They all say one thing: "Fundraising is tough."

FUNDRAISING IS A BIGGER PROBLEM THAN WE REALIZE

YCombinator, one of the most recognized and respected early-stage startup incubators, always knew fundraising was a tedious process that forced founders away from building their businesses to raise capital. To quantify this problem, it built software to connect Series A investors with its startups. The portal tracked various data points for each startup, such as the number of investors the founders interacted with, the number of investors the founders pitched, and the number of rejections before investment offers.

The experiment's results shocked the YCombinator team. Aaron Harris and Janelle Tam from YCombinator published a blog titled *Investor Funnels for Series A's,* where they wrote that "on average, the companies that raised [Series] A's had thirty coffee meetings with individual investors." On average, the founders only secured one term sheet—a document that outlines a venture firm's agreement to invest—out of the thirty initial meetings. Additionally, founders faced a median of eighteen rejections before getting a term sheet. **One company even faced thirty rejections before getting an investment offer.**

Startups that are not funded by YCombinator face even more rejections. In 2019, *Forbes* reported that founders spend between six and nine months fundraising.

The average founder spends at least six months of their startup journey finding the right investors.

Most likely, they spend more time fundraising than YCombinator-backed startups do. Because YCombinator is regarded as one of the top early-stage incubators, other investors trust YCombinator's ability to screen and back the top early-stage startups. Being known as a "YCombinator-backed startup" helps open doors for future fundraising. If YCombinator-backed startups face a median of eighteen rejections, then startups not backed by YCombinator would logically face more rejections.

THE WARM INTRODUCTION

First-time founders who are not a part of prestigious startup incubators like YCombinator most often reach out to investors on their own. Unfortunately, they face difficulties getting responses, because many VCs only respond to inbound requests if they were referred via a known contact. Requiring an introduction to jumpstart an investment conversation is known as a "warm introduction."

Del Johnson, a venture capitalist and lawyer, dedicated the past few years toward discovering ways to reduce the negative impacts of warm introductions. In 2019, Johnson wrote an article titled *Ban Warm Introductions!* which gained significant traction within the venture capital community. After reflecting upon the necessity of warm introductions for quite some time, in his blog post, he asserted, "The truth is, success in our industry often isn't a matter of merit at all, it's a matter of network." Having a contact who works in venture capital makes fundraising much easier, because one introduction can lead to another. Many first-time founders, unfortunately, don't know venture capitalists prior to fundraising. As a result, they don't know someone who can introduce them to the venture capital firm they want to speak with.

Warm introductions can restrict geographically and demographically diverse investments. New VCs can improve returns by not requiring warm introductions.

LOOK BEYOND YOUR BACKYARD

In general, humans create networks within their local communities. When someone first moves into a new neighborhood, they go to meetups, do hobbies, and go to social events to meet new people. Over time, they know more people in their local community than those in a different part of the country they have not yet explored.

Similarly, investors create strong networks with nearby investors. Most likely, a Bay Area investor would have more relationships with other Bay Area investors than they would with Midwest investors. Along with other reasons, an entrepreneur located in the Midwest may have a harder time meeting with a Bay Area investor than a Bay Area founder might. This creates regional hubs, where on average, investors have stronger relationships with founders who are physically close by and weaker ones with those who are not.

Regional networks restrict the visibility that startups in smaller hubs receive. Investors in larger hubs miss out on working with founders in smaller hubs. Every year, Panoramic Ventures, the most active venture capital firm in the state of Georgia according to its website, releases an annual report titled *The State of Startups in the Southeast*. The firm analyzes the Southeast's entrepreneurship ecosystem to discover insights that reflect the region's investing activity. In 2021, they found two key trends:

1. The average investment size in the first half of 2021 is 42 percent greater than what it was in 2020, proving that Georgia startups are raising more capital on average than before.
2. Georgia startups collectively raised more capital in the first six months of 2021 than they did in the entirety of 2020. The state's entrepreneurship ecosystem raised two billion dollars in six months compared to $1.9 billion in the previous twelve months.

Although the COVID-19 pandemic could have lowered VC investments in 2020, the data platform CB Insights discovered that the VC industry invested $130 billion throughout the year, which is an all-time high! Knowing that 2020 was not an anomaly for fundraising makes Georgia's growth even more valid and impressive.

The increase in investments throughout Georgia suggests the state's startups are on track to be more valuable than ever before. If an investor located in another part of the country only networks with investors in their nearby region, then they may not partner with Georgia's startups. As a result, they may miss out on potentially successful deals.

New VCs should listen to investment trends and work with companies outside of their traditional geographic networks.

PROVIDE A SEAT AT THE TABLE

Investors do not only have close ties with those physically close by. They also tend to invest in founders most like them. There is a skewed distribution in ethnicity, gender, and education across VC investors. In 2018, Richard Kerby from Equal Ventures set out to learn whether investors fit a typical stereotype or not. As explained in his *Medium* article titled *Where Did You Go to School?* the investor collected profiles on 1,500 investors and found that:

- 82 percent of the 1,500 investors were males
- 60 percent of the 1,500 investors were white males

Assuming people befriend those most like them, investors may inherently and unconsciously create a strong bias against those who do not fit these profiles, such as women and people of color.

Firms that invest in diverse teams end up generating higher-than-average returns. An impact investing firm called Kapor Capital, based in Oakland, California, prides itself on investing in underrepresented founders. They understand the unique value add that such founders bring to the table. They recall this belief in their *2019 Kapor Capital Impact Report* by proudly stating that "the lived experiences of underrepresented entrepreneurs provide a competitive edge in identifying problems to be solved and markets to be accessed." The data proves this thought process too. Between 2011 and 2017, Kapor Capital generated a higher internal rate of return (IRR) than the industry benchmarks provided by the data companies PitchBook and Cambridge Associates.

- Kapor Capital: 29.02 percent
- Cambridge Associates' Seventy-fifth Percentile: 25.96 percent
- PitchBook's Seventy-fifth Percentile: 26.5 percent

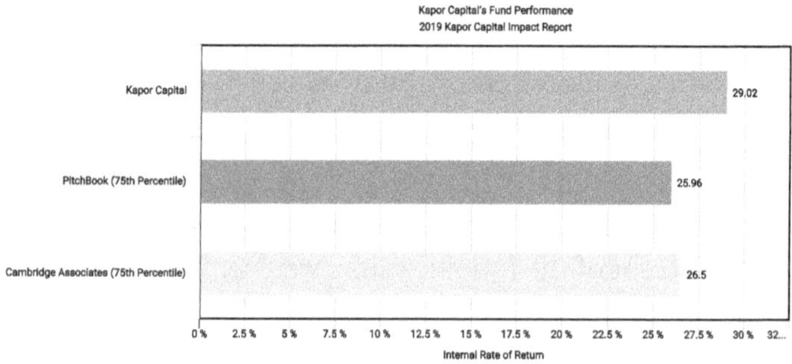

Figure 4 2019 Kapor Capital Report IRR

Over the span of six years, Kapor Capital's portfolio companies, which are led by diverse founders, performed on average better than 75 percent of all other startups.

Kapor Capital is no outlier. Cross Culture Ventures, a Los Angeles-based fifty-million-dollar fund, makes diversity-focused investments. In 2019, the startup newspaper *Tech-Crunch* found that about 72 percent of the VC's portfolio companies' founders are white women or minorities. Over time, three of their portfolio companies exited, and on average, the firm's portfolio's valuation rose by **2,085 percent**.

That is an incredible return.

New VCs should understand that minorities can build successful companies if given the resources they need.

QUICK TECHNIQUE FIRST-TIME FOUNDERS CAN USE

As first-time founders fundraise, they start to pick up on strategies to maximize their chances of meeting investors.

When writing this book, I spoke with Julian Rachman, who founded Ripplink, a student-led startup that helps professionals automate their networking workflow effortlessly. The ambitious entrepreneur founded his startup when he was a student at the University of California at Irvine and built a team to tackle the problem of business software communication.

When he started to fundraise, Rachman was shocked by its difficulty. He told me other founders sent investors emails with long paragraphs explaining every aspect of their startup. Unfortunately, in the interest of time, investors may not read lengthy emails, no matter how great the startup is.

To increase his response rate, Rachman sent a short email that showed:

- His short bio

- His startup's description
- His startup's traction

He sent the following cold email to investors:

> *"Hello, my name is Julian. This is a TLDR about me and my company*
>
> *Student founder, started Ripplink, team of six, two amazing advisers*
>
> *100 percent bootstrapped, 300 people on waitlist, releasing app in two weeks"*

New VCs may appreciate the email template's brevity and conciseness, which can improve first-time founders' chances of receiving responses.

KEY LESSONS TO BECOMING DATA-DRIVEN

- Fundraising requires at least six months of founders' lives. It's a massive pain point in VC.
- Diverse founders may outperform the rest of the industry.
- Invest in startups outside a traditional geographic region.

***

The three biggest motivations to **becoming data-driven** are:

- Too much manual work
- Broken data on startups and VCs
- A lack of diversity in VC investments

In the next section, we will embark on a **Journey to Becoming Data-Driven** by exploring the steps data-driven VCs and data scientists should take.

2

THE JOURNEY TO BECOMING DATA-DRIVEN

CHAPTER 5

Decide to Become Data-Driven

One of my biggest fears is that new VCs will begin to invest significant resources in building data science teams and infrastructure without clearly understanding how to execute a data science plan, or worse yet, not knowing if they even need data science.

To decide whether data science is right for you—think first, then act.

THINK FIRST, THEN ACT

Data science in venture capital is an emerging field. Only a few have successfully dabbled with it. One of these thought leaders is Jonathan Hsu. He and I spoke about his journey, learnings, and advice.

Before exploring the intersection between data science and venture capital, the University of California at Berkeley and

Stanford University alum told me he spent years building technology companies. He first started, scaled, and sold one of the first-ever social gaming companies to Slide, a Bay Area company run by Max Levchin, one of the founders of PayPal. Hsu eventually made his way to Facebook, where he helped create and lead its data science and analytics division and grew the team from six to 150 people. After developing a strong interest in venture investing, Hsu decided to join Social Capital, where he worked with prominent and influential investors such as Chamath Palihapitiya and explored the relationship between data science and venture capital. A few years later, he and some others from Social Capital transitioned over to start their own firm called Tribe Capital, where they use data analytics to measure early-stage product-market fit.

Hsu's years of experience in startups and venture capital taught him that data and the firm's investment thesis should be independent of each other. He explained to me that too many firms make the mistake of conflating the two. He specifically advised, "Data science and technology in investing is not a substitute for an investment thesis." **Companies need first to develop their own investment thesis and then determine if data science really is the best way to implement it.**

Hsu narrated an example that contextualizes the lesson. Suppose an investment firm believes that talent is the most important indicator of a startup's success. To measure a startup's talent, traditionally, investors would meet founders, learn more about their backgrounds, such as work history and education, and then decide whether they want to pursue the conversation. They may refer to technology to implement and scale their thesis by deciding to partner with LinkedIn to access its data securely and ethically. Then, they can draw insights that instantly reflect the quality of the startup's talent. In this case, the firm already believed that talent was the best indicator and then sought ways to quickly gather information about the startup's talent.

An investor who believes talent is most important might immediately, as Hsu described, "look at the data behind a startup's talent because they believe, rightly or wrongly, that the only thing that matters is talent."

The problem is that the investor is making two steps at once:

- The investor is making the investment thesis about a startup's talent.
- The investor is using technology—specifically data—to express the investment thesis.

They immediately incorrectly assume that data is the **best** way to reflect a startup's talent. Rather, the investor should:

1. Create an investment thesis.
2. Explore all the ways that reflect the quality of the start-up's talent.
3. Compare them.
4. Determine if data really is the most impactful method.

Clearly defining the problem statement, comparing potential solutions, and implementing the most impactful solution is not unique to venture. In general, businesses first identify their strategy and then decide whether and how they should use technology to implement it. When Hsu worked at Facebook, he noticed the social media firm greatly prioritized developing the best product experience possible. The team then decided that data could most greatly improve the product, so they hired many data scientists, engineers, and product managers. Similarly, Hsu told me that Slack, which is a business-to-business software company, prioritizes acquiring sales contracts. Hence, their analytics and data science teams discover methods to optimize sales.

Hsu gave credit where it's due. He clarified that Benjamin Graham, an economist who has been coined as the "father of value investing," first inspired the idea of looking at companies objectively. Graham published two influential books that shaped neoclassical investing: *Security Analysis* and *The Intelligent Investor*. Hsu told me that in the 1930s, Graham was the first to popularize using financial statements to make investment decisions. Although that sounds obvious, before the 1930s, people often invested based on nonfinancial factors, such as the fear of missing out (FOMO) and rumors. Only business owners and managers used financial statements to improve their own operations. Graham had a specific thesis around value and an implementation of that thesis revolving around ascertaining book value from financial statements and using that as a core guide to investment decisions.

Hsu and his co-founders implemented the same philosophy at Tribe Capital. The team's philosophy is to "understand the signal objectively and use different frameworks to achieve that." For them, their signal is product-market fit, and over the years, they developed different ways to measure a startup's engagement and traction with the few data points that early-stage startups provide. The framework that Hsu describes has been successfully deployed over several years at both Social Capital and Tribe Capital to invest in prolific companies such as Slack, Carta, Front, and Bolt.

KEY LESSONS TO BECOMING DATA-DRIVEN
- Develop a thesis around what you think best signals a startup's success. If your approach requires technology, then invest in building the right infrastructure and tools.
- Do not search whether a technique can solve a problem. Rather, first, find the problem and then determine if the technique is the best possible solution.
- Look at companies objectively.

CHAPTER 6

Build Your Own Data

———

We know we can't exclusively use public data. We must track our own data. Creating an entirely data-driven VC can seem incredibly daunting. One person who turned this theoretical idea into an actual product is Will Bricker. VCs who want to be data-driven can and should apply Bricker's learnings within their own firms.

Bricker worked at Bridgewater Associates, the world's largest hedge fund, where he collaborated with pre-seed startups that built tools for finance firms. Researching and understanding the startups' struggles gradually made Bricker interested in entrepreneurship. After he earned his Master's in Business Administration from the University of California at Berkeley, Bricker began to work at the Hustle Fund, one of the Bay Area's most respected early-stage venture capital firms, where he applied his quantitative analysis skills and data-driven background.

VENTURE SYSTEMIZATION

Bricker quickly identified the biggest difference between public and private markets: data availability. When I spoke to him, he told me about the framework he developed to track and utilize the Hustle Fund's internal, proprietary data: **venture systemization.** He broke the framework down into two parts:

1. Build operational visibility and value <u>today</u>.
2. Lay the foundations to scale the system <u>tomorrow</u>.

Ideally, VCs should access a platform that tracks every single metric for every startup in real-time, like how public market investors can look at trading platforms, such as Bloomberg Terminal or Robinhood. Until the private markets have this system, VCs can leverage what Bricker calls "data creativity" to track the data they need. He open-sourced his research with recommendations for new VCs to implement:

1. Rationalize current flows.
    a. Write down what you currently do daily.
    b. Reflect on what processes and data points you believe are most important.
2. Strategize ways to collect important data.
    a. Envision what an ideal system looks like.
    b. Outline inexpensive and quick solutions to capture valuable data.
3. Showcase the newly built system's value.

When rationalizing current flows, new VCs will learn what data they currently interact with but may not track. For example, they may learn that they:

- Mostly communicate with founders over email.
- Store the pitch decks on their local computers.
- Prefer founders with deep, personal missions.

Now, the investors know their most common routines and values. The VC also now knows where to collect data from: email communications, locally stored data, and personal missions.

When strategizing ways to collect the most important data, the VC may realize that emails and pitch decks are tangible sources of information, but personal missions may be difficult to quantify. Because the VC can quickly aggregate data from emails and semistructured files, it may want to prioritize that first and then quantify the personal mission data.

Once investors build systems that automatically collect data from emails and pitch decks, then they can visualize analytics for leadership. For example, the VC may track the number of startups it talks to, how frequently it communicates with startups it funds versus doesn't fund, and the total time spent to decide whether to fund a startup. It can finally improve time management by learning if it spends too much time reviewing startups it does not fund.

In this case, the current deal flow statistics serve as the short-term value, and the data-driven time management strategies provide the long-term value. This embodies Bricker's biggest advice for VCs trying to become more data-driven: **structure data capturing methods** and **figure out ways to use them to make lives easier right now.**

Bricker told me an analogy that helps put this framework into perspective.

If someone were to ask themself, "On a scale of one to ten, how healthy am I?" they may need to look at many different factors. Ideally, they can analyze the sequencing of all their genetics to detect every healthy and malicious cell they have and find any current and upcoming diseases. However, that process does not commonly exist.

Just because doctors don't have a single test that can predict every disease their patients will get does not mean that the doctors give up. Rather, they compile information about different features, such as height, weight, physical fitness, and other biological indicators, to estimate their patients' overall health. They don't just do one test. They perform as many tests on as many different body parts and biological systems as they reasonably can, so they have enough data points to determine whether their patients are healthy. For example, measuring the patients' weight tells them if the patients are overweight or underweight. That one data point on its own is not enough to evaluate the patient's entire health. Doctors examine other parts of the body, too, such as the cardiovascular system, nervous system, and immune system.

When beginning to become data-driven, VCs might not have a portal that shows the real-time statistics of their operations, like how doctors don't have an accurate genetic sequencing algorithm that immediately measures a patient's health. However, VCs can ask themselves, "What data exists?" and "How can I use that existing data to determine my VC's health?" to develop immediate operational value and long-term data-driven solutions and analytics.

Venture systemization works. Bricker's techniques helped the Hustle Fund enable 40 percent of all deals to be handled without human intervention.

Venture systemization gives VCs back the one resource they cannot control: time.

QUANTIFY INTANGIBLE DATA

In the example above, the email communications and pitch decks are tangible data sources. VCs can immediately create summary statistics, such as the number of emails sent to a founder or the length of persuasive pitch decks. Although VCs may not immediately know how to quantify the founder's personal missions, they should start tracking them because personal missions can predict startup success and add incredible value to the VC's proprietary dataset.

I recently met a founder, whom we'll call John Doe, who lost his entire family—his wife and two beautiful kids—in a terrible car accident. They passed away before they could receive medical attention.

Only Doe survived.

Doe was so shaken by what happened that he founded a startup that predicts traffic accidents before they occur. He worked with local traffic stations to access real-time traffic camera footage. After compiling millions of videos, his team built machine learning models to understand the car positions seconds before they get into an accident. Once it identifies a potential accident, it automatically alerts the police to dispatch for help and the local healthcare professionals to prepare for the incident.

His core reason to found his startup was to make sure no one else had to lose loved ones like he did.

After hearing his story, VCs would see why Doe is so determined to make his startup a success. If data-driven VCs had a quantifiable score for the founders' personal investment and devotion, then he should get full marks.

When talking to startups, new VCs should ask deeper, personal questions and document their answers. Instead of just asking generic questions about the startup's market share and competitors, they should learn why the founders started the company. This provides unique insight into the founder's spiritual relationship to the problem they are trying to solve.

Personal motivation with the startup's product can predict startup success. Tim Brady, a current partner at YCombinator and a co-founder of the powerful search engine Yahoo, believes that humans can easily detect inauthenticity. During a YCombinator lecture titled *Building Culture,* he explained that sometimes founders "choose an idea because it sounds good to tell their friends at a party," but when times get tough, "it's really hard to maintain that level of energy." He later said that a few years ago, a YCombinator participant joined the program to help various retailers liquidate their excess inventory. Eventually, the startup pivoted and sold only makeup for teenage girls. Unfortunately, according to Brady, the founder didn't "identify with the problem," and his employees took notice. One day in the office, they walked up to him and told him, "Hey, like, it doesn't look like you're enjoying what you're doing." After realizing that the founders didn't have a personal connection to the pain point, the employees lost interest in their work, and the founder shut the company down.

New VCs can utilize Bricker's framework of venture systemization to track and quantify founders' stories.

When they rationalize their current processes, VCs can learn how they got in contact with the founder and what they did after meeting them. For example, they may learn:

- Sources of lead generation (referral, cold email, networking event, etc.);
- Due diligence before meeting the founder (whether they used the product, read online reviews, read the founder's LinkedIn page, etc.);
- Questions asked during the founder meeting (market share, competitive strategy, personal mission, etc.); and
- Postmeeting actions (followed up over email, read over the pitch deck two more times, etc.).

When strategizing ways to collect important data, VCs may learn that they unconsciously measure the personal missions based on the founders' vocabulary, body language, and emotions. This may motivate VCs to transcribe the meeting notes and record the audio (if the founder agrees and the audio stays confidential) during startup pitches.

In the short-term, VCs can share the transcribed notes with all meeting attendees.

To develop long-term business value, VCs can:

- Compare the vocabulary used by founders to assess and differentiate the entrepreneurs who have strong personal missions versus those who do not. VCs can use natural language processing algorithms like term-frequency inverse-document-frequency (TFIDF) to generate a list of words that indicate strong personal missions for VCs to look for during startup pitches.
- Measure how passionate founders are based on how quickly they speak. If VCs realize that they believe passionate founders speak quickly, then they can leverage dynamic time warping to measure the number of words spoken per minute. They can quantify the founder's passion by comparing their words spoken per minute against a benchmark.

In this case, the system's short-term value is immediately creating and sharing the meeting notes. The long-term value is the data-driven score that determines whether a founder has a strong personal mission.

KEY LESSONS TO BECOMING DATA-DRIVEN
- Start documenting data you did not previously track.

- Write down daily processes to clarify values and discover potential data sources.
- When choosing which products to build, optimize for speed.
- Deliver short-term operational value that creates the groundwork for long-term products.
- Quantify intangible data, such as founders' personal missions, to build proprietary data.

CHAPTER 7

Leverage Crowdsourced Data

Think like a startup.

Hypergrowth startups don't just rely on one source of revenue. They maximize their chances of finding product-market fit by building multiple products. Similarly, VCs shouldn't depend on one technique to collect data. They should strategize ways to aggregate as much high-quality data in as little time as possible.

To diversify data collection from multiple sources, new VCs should consider crowdsourcing information on startups and industries. Investopedia defines crowdsourcing as the process of "obtaining work, information, or opinions from a large group of people who submit their data." VCs are no stranger to using crowdsourced data. In 2018, Crunchbase released a statement on its *User Privacy* website page stating it collects information on individuals, organizations, and users by asking volunteers to submit data. Along with other data collection techniques, such as documenting user interactions, Crunchbase developed data collection systems to share information on more than one million companies.

Although investors should continue using Crunchbase, it may not exclusively provide a competitive advantage—other VCs can also access the same preprocessed and standardized data. Generating proprietary insights on unique investment opportunities requires leveraging other crowdsourced, raw, and unstructured data that non-data-driven VCs may not recognize. Before new data-driven investors embark on this journey, they first need to learn what techniques did and did not work for other crowdsourced data platforms.

OWLER'S STARTUP ADVENTURE

Owler, a Bay Area-based startup that sold for $24.5 million to Meltwater in 2021, set out on a mission to democratize access to data on companies across industries.

I spoke directly with Owler's Chief Executive Officer, Tim Harsch. He told me that the company crowdsourced enough data to analyze more than thirteen million companies and attract more than 3.5 million monthly logins. Sales and marketing teams and institutional investors utilize his platform to learn insider insights and make better business decisions.

Prior to co-founding Owler, Harsch worked at a contact crowdsourcing startup called Jigsaw, where he internalized how valuable and scalable crowdsourcing can be. Harsch informed me that at the time, there were very few sources of company information. Only Dun and Bradstreet, an organization that has been around for almost two hundred years, shared company data. After realizing the massive opportunity, he and two other people from Jigsaw, Jim Fowler and Rajan Madhavan, went on to start Owler together.

During the ten years between the company's inception and acquisition, Owler iterated over different products. Harsch told me that Owler pivoted based on learnings they gathered over time.

Harsch explained that at first, Owler paid industry outsiders, many of whom were university students and professional analysts, to research certain markets. The team at Owler envisioned that the researchers would aggregate data from multiple sources and write coherent and detailed reports on the assigned industries. After spending about a quarter of a million dollars, the team conceded that the strategy did not work for two reasons:

1. The chicken-and-egg problem
2. Vague data

The chicken-and-egg problem—The product composed of two sides: the supply side (the reports the researchers wrote) and the demand side (customers who wanted the reports). To justify writing additional reports, Owler needed to sell many existing reports, but the customers were not interested in just some reports—they wanted significantly more reports to keep paying for the platform! Owler could not hire more researchers without customers guaranteeing they would buy the analysis. The mismatch between the supply and demand did not warrant an additional investment of resources.

Vague data—The reports' authors did not work in the industry. The writers summarized existing online market reports. As a result, their findings were not as insightful as customers hoped.

After many iterations, Owler now gives users free access to the platform if they periodically answer questions about their professions' industries. For example, when collecting data on self-driving cars, Owler would talk to employees from Waymo, a startup building autonomous vehicles. Similarly, when Owler wants to learn about the food supply chain industry, it would ask employees of Imperfect Foods, a subscription service for fresh produce.

Harsch told me, "This new business model focuses on people sharing little bits of knowledge they have, and Owler putting the data together into a cohesive format."

The new crowdsourcing format shows the value and importance of communities. Harsch told me that community-driven data sharing could be beneficial for three reasons:

1. **Exclusive access to data**
2. **Scalable**
3. **Avoids biased data**

Exclusive access to data—Owler gets access to data other companies don't have.

Harsch told me that until fifteen years ago, all data collection was manual. Companies hired thousands of people globally to manually gather data by calling and mailing companies with questionnaires and surveys. Since then, data companies realized they could leverage technology to collect information more efficiently. They implemented techniques to crawl websites safely, legally, and ethically. Web scraping technologies accelerated and magnified the amount of data they could ingest. Unfortunately, they could only collect the information physically found on websites. They could not get the "inside scoop" that customers wanted.

While Owler does have an internal data team that uses technology to compile external data quickly, the company, as Harsch described, "found its magic" by building and leveraging a community to get exclusive access to data other companies don't have. **They found that employees gave more specific and detailed company information than online market reports**.

Scalable—Manually collecting data from websites is tedious. Harsch emphasized that traditional organizations need "literally thousands of people in rooms" to collect data by hand. Technology, on the other hand, greatly reduced the number of resources needed to get the same data.

Avoids biased data—Harsch identifies one of the data industry's biggest problems to be organizations aggregating each other's data and not correcting for each source's underlying biases. Many companies buy other organizations' data, merge them, and sell the combined data. Customers may initially trust the data, but over time, doubt creeps in. For example, a data source might accurately display information for early-stage education startups but not for early-stage transportation logistics startups. After realizing the inconsistent data quality, customers may begin to ask themselves, "The data vendor has good data for industry X, but is it credible for industry Y?"

Owler's mantra of quality over quantity and emphasis on community-building helps provide customers with valuable data they may not see elsewhere. Owler complements the data science techniques, such as web scraping and data cleaning, with human touches by asking its community company-specific and industry-specific questions. Many investors trust Owler's data for good reason—they created high-quality profiles for more than thirteen million organizations!

CREATE DATA FROM CROWDSOURCED PLATFORMS

VCs may want to develop communities of startups and ask questions about industry trends. For example, a VC can create a portal for its portfolio companies to share industry insights they recognize, which may help VCs better understand which future trends to invest in. Harsch advised me on three lessons he learned at Owler that he believes future crowdsourced data platforms should implement:

1. **Gather as much data from as many people and sectors as possible**—Having many data sources de-risks the likelihood of Owler showcasing poor or inaccurate data.
2. **Ask easily answerable yet specific enough questions for the answers to be useful**—People who provide content are busy and do not want to spend too much time answering questions.
3. **Build trust with the respondents**—Emphasize data quality over data quantity and do not force answers

from anyone. Harsch said that sometimes, Owler would ask questions to someone who works in the right role at the right company, but they are uncomfortable sharing any data. Do not pressurize them. Other times, people may be willing to distribute information, but they may work in the incorrect role or be unqualified to answer the questions. If the data they provide is wrong, then Owler's data becomes wrong too. Do not think that more data is better data.

If VCs do not want to build their own communities, then they can investigate structuring information from existing data hubs, such as Reddit. The social networking site contains a plethora of customer-generated data that reflects public opinions on industries and problems. According to a whitepaper released by Backlinko, an SEO marketing site, Reddit users posted two billion comments in 2020 alone. Almost a quarter of all US adults use Reddit. An impressive 430 million active users engage with the platform monthly. The forum shows crowdsourced data from users worldwide, making it the perfect data source to learn the public's opinions about certain issues. VCs can partner with Reddit to access its data safely and ethically.

For example, if a startup wants to solve traffic congestion in a specific city, then VCs can read Reddit's transportation-related or city-related forums and measure how frequently users complain about traffic. If people frequently voice annoyances and inconveniences, then VCs may consider it as a legitimate and urgent problem needed to be solved.

Investors would need to correct for any biases in Reddit or other crowdsourced platforms' data. For example, a VC may hypothesize that comments with the most engagement represent how the community collectively feels about the issue. However, the most popular comment may be sarcastic or offensive. The VCs should remove biased information from their dataset. Keeping only objective data that accurately represents the community's point of view embodies Harsch's mantra of quality over quantity.

Data-driven investors can implement novel data collection and manipulation techniques to analyze unstructured, crowdsourced data and learn of new problems and potential investment opportunities quickly.

KEY LESSONS TO BECOMING DATA-DRIVEN

- Leverage technology to collect data as quickly and accurately as possible.
- Compile the dataset from individuals with relevant industry experience. Don't only rely on building the dataset from other research reports.
- Examine how similar data vendors collect their data. Do not use biased data.
- Invest resources in standardizing public, crowdsourced data that other investors may not look at.

CHAPTER 8

Create Your Data Team

———

New VCs must hire data teams to build and execute their data strategy. The first data hire will most likely face unexpected challenges. This book helps data scientists overcome such situations. I met with other first data hires, gathered their feedback, and summarized their lessons, so future data hires don't feel isolated or lost.

I spoke with Beiming Liu, who worked as Crunchbase's first data scientist and developed many of Crunchbase's data-driven products. Liu joined Crunchbase in 2018 when between eighty and ninety employees worked for the firm. Over time, he evolved the company to embody a data-driven culture and implement machine learning models across its business practices.

It wasn't always easy, though. He told me he faced three challenges he believes future data scientists in VC need to prepare for:

- Align expectations with stakeholders and colleagues.
- Creating training data can be harder than it seems.

- Models might not work as expected.

THE ROLE OF THE FIRST DATA SCIENTIST

ALIGN EXPECTATIONS WITH STAKEHOLDERS AND COLLEAGUES.
Liu told me people often think machine learning can magically solve all their business problems. Although they may be joking, he finds that people do have high expectations. When Liu started at Crunchbase, many of his colleagues had previously heard of machine learning and data science, but they didn't know its details or use cases. As a result, Liu's first challenge was to communicate and advocate what machine learning can and cannot technically and ethically solve.

For example, when Crunchbase users create new startup profiles, they sometimes accidentally leave the startups' industries blank or include the incorrect industries. Users cannot easily find startups with incorrect or empty industry fields. Liu told me, "Predicting the industry or category of a company based on the company's information, like its descriptions, competitors, or products, is possible." Data teams can:

1. Collect each startup's description;
2. Collect each startup's correct industry; and
3. Create a supervised machine learning model to predict the startup's correct industry based on the words found in the description.

Other project ideas can be technically feasible yet unethical. For example, Liu told me he could technically create a model that predicts when a startup is likely to announce its next fundraising date. This informs investors which startups are fundraising. However, not all founders may want to publicize their expected fundraising timeline, as such notifications can alert their competitors, or the startups might not actually be ready to fundraise. Data hires need to consider their projects' ethical implications.

Additionally, data scientists need to help stakeholders understand their predictive models' accuracies. Liu told me, "People think of technology as black magic, but rarely do people think about how the training data is used to develop these products." Going back to the industry predictor model mentioned above, Liu said he could create a model that correctly classifies a startup's industry about 85 to 90 percent of the time. It may be unreasonable to expect the classifier to work 100 percent correctly. **If the model correctly classifies a startup's industry more accurately than a human can, then leadership should consider the project as a win.**

If stakeholders still want to make the model more accurate, then data scientists can request for additional resources to improve the underlying data's quality. Data scientists need to phrase their ask correctly to maximize the chance they get their requested resources. Liu's go-to phrasing is, "If we spend X dollars, then we can improve our data quality by Y percent, which can lead to a Z percent increase in model performance. That means we can correctly predict the startup's industry Z percent more accurately than currently." Contextualizing model performance to business value helps stakeholders understand whether the additional investment justifies the potential impact.

To align internal expectations, leadership and data scientists can work together to identify machine learning's feasibilities, understand model accuracies, and improve underlying data quality.

CREATING TRAINING DATA IS HARDER THAN IT SEEMS.
Suppose that in the earlier example, leadership approves the request to invest in higher-quality data. The data leader can either buy existing data or collect new data.

Given there are not many comprehensive venture capital datasets available for sale, Liu would have to train a team to build his own labeled data. He must write a training guide, hire a data entry team, and ensure consistency across the dataset. To start this project, he might look at a few hundred startups' descriptions, label the correct industries, and write in a training guide why he believes the listed industry is the correct industry. Each team member would then follow the instructions to label more industries. His predictive model can learn additional relationships if it is trained on more data, allowing it to perform better on new, unseen data.

Standardizing industry labels for all startups is the key to building a high-quality, proprietary dataset. He worked with data managers to monitor the data labeling process. Liu told me that, in general, people often mislabel data points for a variety of reasons:

- People can be rushed between deadlines.
- People get fatigued after labeling data for many hours.

- Unclear training guides can make people label based on their own judgment. One person might label the same data differently than another would.

Over time, Liu found ways to reduce the number of errors made. Prescreening data labelers improved the process the most. He told me he would ask the labelers ten or twenty questions to learn how they would label the data. He would show a few examples and ask them to label it. If they got all ten or twenty questions correct, then Liu would be confident in their labeling abilities. If they mislabeled the data, however, then he would prepare additional documents and ask the data managers to retrain the data labelers.

Understanding the sources of mislabeled data can help data scientists prevent bad data labeling in the future. Once the data scientist feels confident in the dataset's quality, then they can proceed to make the model. First, data hires need to create training guides, establish the relationships with data managers, and implement proactive solutions to prevent bad data labeling.

MODELS MIGHT NOT WORK AS EXPECTED.
Even after improving the underlying data, the model might not work. This might be disappointing and stressful, but Liu encourages data scientists to think differently.

First, they should not be discouraged. If anything, they should explore other types of algorithms that may work better. Once the underlying data changes, the model should change too. For example, if an original dataset had two thousand observations, but after the team labels additional data, there are now ten thousand observations, then the model for the first dataset might not work as well as it would for the second dataset. Some machine learning algorithms work better on smaller datasets, while others work better on larger ones. Liu refers to this phenomenon as the "no free lunch" principle. **No single algorithm can solve all problems**, which explains why many types of algorithms exist. If only one model solved all business problems, then only one type of machine learning algorithm would exist.

Second, Liu thinks data scientists should view solving machine learning problems in terms of iterations. If the model does not work at first, then they should go back to the training data, find potential sources of errors, such as optimizing the model on the wrong metrics or incorporating poor data quality, and then refine the model. Repeating this process can improve the model's accuracy.

If the model is still not as accurate as expected, then data scientists should move on. Liu said, "In an ideal world, the team may have all the data and engineering resources they need to implement a quality machine learning pipeline, but they might not have that at a startup [or venture capital firm]. It is okay to tell the manager the project didn't go as expected by first outlining what the team attempted then explaining why they didn't work." Data scientists should strive to still improve the models as much as possible, but if they cannot improve them any further, then leadership may empathize and encourage the team to move on to the next project.

Liu launching impactful data products within the venture ecosystem, such as engines that suggest which startups Crunchbase users should explore based on their interests, proves data teams can leverage machine learning for venture capital. Liu's experiences as a first data hire shows future data hires how to work with leadership to demonstrate business value.

HIRING QUALIFIED DATA SCIENTISTS

Once the first data hire successfully proves data's value and potential, they may also hire additional members to the team. Each new hire needs to possess certain qualifications to be successful in venture capital.

Henry Apfel, a former member of PitchBook's data team, spent three years learning the ins and outs of the data business. He and I discussed his journey in VC data.

He told me the private market industry can be a secluded bubble that is difficult to understand from the outside. Once a data scientist enters the VC space, they need to think through two lenses simultaneously: as a venture capitalist and as a data scientist.

Data scientists can build the venture capital lens by:

- Reading the firm's meeting notes and investment memos for startups in the due diligence pipeline;
- Networking with investors and understanding their perspectives on current industry trends;
- Consuming the many investment blogs that VCs publish;

- Scrolling through the threads that investors post on Twitter;
- Devouring forward-looking market reports about the industries the VC invests in;
- Understanding the process of business development, negotiating, and signing deals with external data vendors; and
- Thinking of key performance indicators (KPIs) to demonstrate the team's impact.

From a data perspective, **data scientists need to stop thinking in terms of big data and start thinking in terms of small data.** Apfel told me that unlike public markets and large technology firms, "you don't have the ten trillion rows of perfectly arranged and perfectly organized data that's constantly streaming into a massive data system."

Apfel explained that data scientists need to "get used to a dataset that might be one hundred or one thousand or ten thousand rows!"

Despite the limited data, candidates need to successfully answer questions like:

- "What can I do with this data?"
- "What are the useful conclusions I can draw from here?"

Making small data useful tests a data scientist's knowledge of statistical inferencing and domain-specific context. Apfel believes although statistical inference may not be as glamorous as machine learning, it is extremely important and necessary, nonetheless. Think of it as the backbone of machine learning.

Data scientists can make small data useful if they can defend their statistical tests and analysis. When choosing which test to use, Apfel suggests data scientists:

- Look at each assumption they make;
- Validate each assumption; and
- Determine whether each assumption is reasonable.

Let us assume that a data scientist has been asked to determine whether the number of years of a founder's prior work experience affects the startup's success. They will need to measure the feature's statistical significance, meaning whether the feature is important enough to affect the test's outcome. The data scientist plans to use a "T-test," which is one of the most foundational statistical tests. The test assumes there is an equal number of observations in each group: successful and failed startups. Suppose the data scientist has access to information on the outcomes for one hundred companies but immediately notices that 70 percent of the companies succeeded and 30 percent failed. To avoid concluding incorrect results, the data scientist stops using this test and moves on to the next possible one.

The data scientist followed Apfel's suggestion:

1. Look at each assumption the team is making—They considered each assumption that T-tests require.
2. Validate the assumption—They saw an unequal number of observations in each group.

3. Determine whether their assumption is reasonable—They decided it was unreasonable to continue because the unequal number of observations would skew the results, so they moved on to the next test.

After completing the statistical analysis, they need to explain their results to leadership. Data scientists cannot expect stakeholders to understand the nitty-gritty behind statistics. Rather, they need to explain their approach at a high-level so leadership can spend more time deciding strategic action items rather than understanding the analysis. Apfel suggests presenting a three-step framework to leadership:

- Explain what is happening.
- Explain what each assumption means.
- Describe how the output would change depending on whether each assumption is true or false.

The project can be considered successful once leadership understands the data's story and finalizes the next actionable steps. VCs should look for data scientists who can make small data usable and communicate their results to leadership.

HIT SINGLES AND DOUBLES BEFORE GOING FOR THE GRAND SLAM

Of course, this is all easier said than done.

We can evangelize the importance of data and showcase the benefits all day long. However, we need to ensure stakeholders can trust the data team with hundreds of thousands of dollars—or even millions of dollars—in resources.

That doesn't happen overnight.

Mini experiments can showcase data's business value and build a strong case for additional resources. Instead of immediately creating the most interesting and comprehensive predictive model, data scientists can automate simpler data tasks or analyses that the company already manually performs.

For example, venture capital firms often fly globally to meet limited partners and startups. At the end of the year, the firm calculates operational expenses. Currently, the accounting team may aggregate receipts and manually store the costs in a spreadsheet. This may lead to data entry errors. A data scientist, however, can use computer vision to scan and extract the data from all the receipts, create a web app that displays the firm's expenses, and share the app with the team. The finance team would no longer need to spend long hours manually going through receipts and calculating all the expenses. Technology can automate financial operations with fewer errors. A project like this showcases technology's potential and shows leadership that the data scientist can build similar products that save time and prevent bad data entry.

Similarly, reviewing legal documents, such as startups' articles of incorporations and investment memos, takes many hours. Both analysts and legal teams read them many times before approving them. Data scientists can leverage natural language processing models to identify key phrases that the documents should and should not include. This helps the analysts and legal teams automatically know which parts of the documents they should pay extra attention to.

Data scientists at finance firms do not have to solve the hardest problems first. Rather, they can build mini products, collect data over time, and build enough credibility with leadership to eventually build their dream team. Or, in baseball terms, data scientists should focus on small wins—singles and doubles—before tackling the firm's hardest data problems—hitting a grand slam.

KEY LESSONS TO BECOMING DATA-DRIVEN
- Facilitate transparent conversations with leadership to align expectations.
- Invest in resources to improve the underlying data by hiring a data labeling team to create more training data.
- Communicate why a data project did or did not work.
- Work on projects that deliver short-term impact before working on more risky, long-term projects.
- Hire data scientists based on their statistical inferencing abilities.

***

In this next section, we will learn the **Data-Driven Investing Techniques** that other data-driven investors implement to build competitive advantages.

3

DATA-DRIVEN INVESTING TECHNIQUES

CHAPTER 9

Remove Bias

We all have biases.

If you drive a car and get into a car accident, then you might not want to drive for a while. If you eat at a restaurant and previously heard many reviews about a specific dish, then you may be compelled to order it. If you wait in a long line for a roller coaster and see people leave because they are tired of waiting, then you might want to continue to stay in line because you already spent enough time waiting so you might as well reap the benefit.

Venture capital is no different.

Many systematic flaws filtered through the lens of cognitive biases can lead to poor assumptions and judgments about entrepreneurs, market trends, and investments. The inability to identify and correct these biases blinds many venture investors from making well-informed decisions.

I spoke with Clint Korver, an entrepreneur turned investor and Stanford University alumnus, who exclaimed to me,

"Venture capital could be the poster child for cognitive bias."
Through his eyes, bias is omnipresent and inevitable.

SOURCES OF BIAS IN VC

Over his investing career, Korver identified three main biases
within venture:

- Confirmation bias—An investor ignores disconfirming
  evidence.
- Cultural-driven bias—An investor uses various lenses for
  entrepreneurs from different ethnic backgrounds.
- Availability bias—An investor excludes many industry
  sectors and disproportionately gives spotlight to one or
  two sectors.

Investors display confirmation biases by listening to what
they want to hear and ignoring everything else. In fact, they
actively seek and prioritize information that supports theories they already had. For example, if an investor strongly
believes that founders from top public schools or Ivy League
universities make the best entrepreneurs, then they might
ignore all the evidence that suggests otherwise and instead
reject all entrepreneurs who do not have a similar educa-
tional background.

In availability bias, according to Korver, people compare
everything to current, popular trends. For example, Korver noticed that startups brand themselves as "Uber for
X" or "Airbnb for Y" because everyone can relate to Uber
and Airbnb. He also told me that up to about ten or fifteen
years ago, computer science dropouts from top universities

received the most attention and venture backing. But when Airbnb attracted significant attention, the narrative suddenly shifted. Instead of partnering with computer science dropouts, VCs looked for founders who were designers because the Airbnb founders were designers from the Rhode Island School of Design.

Korver clarified that VCs should not not invest in designers. Rather, immediately shifting their thesis away from investing in computer science dropouts to investing in designers excmplifies a systematically incomplete idea of what investors should look for in founders. It excludes opportunities to invest in other amazing founders or innovative sectors not currently in the spotlight.

Although eliminating biases completely may seem impossible, new VCs can take actionable steps to mitigate such preferences and make venture capital more equitable. **Removing biases from their data helps VCs become more data-driven because they start to make informed decisions on objective data, not subjective data.**

REMOVE BIAS IN DUE DILIGENCE

Korver, a four-time author, partnered with Miriam Rivera, a former Google attorney and Stanford Law School alum, to start Ulu Ventures, a seed-stage investment firm that invested in leading companies such as Palintir and SoFi. They strive to remove as much cognitive bias from venture capital as possible. In fact, Korver told me their motto is "to be systematic in thinking through the risk and overcoming the cognitive bias" they see when evaluating deals.

Korver and Rivera noticed that investors display the most cognitive biases to entrepreneurs based on their personal backgrounds. Just like any other investors, they attended many startup pitches, demo days, and coffee chats. Over time, they realized that venture capitalists ask female founders different questions than male founders. Korver specified that, in his experience, "Venture capitalists ask women about downside protection and men about upside potential." Using different questions based on the founders' backgrounds **screams** bias!

Ulu Ventures decided to ask every founder the same questions—no matter their background.

The Ulu team writes down their decision criteria—the standards they use to determine whether to invest in a startup—so they cannot change their criteria later. To keep themselves accountable and stay transparent, they even published the decision criteria online. Maintaining their standards regardless of the founder's background solves the cultural-driven bias.

Korver and Rivera also understand they view the world differently from each other. They both have their own cultural differences. As Korver puts it, one co-founder is a "White man," and the other co-founder is a "Hispanic woman." Coming from different ethnic and gender backgrounds only makes them stronger partners. When examining startups, the two have in-depth, thorough conversations that highlight perspectives the other person might not have thought of. Korver believes having an investing team with only one culture's point of view can lead to false judgments about entrepreneurs.

After speaking with the startup founders many times, the Ulu team sits down and measures the startup's probability of success. Some investors believe that if a startup excels in one or two areas, then it will eventually be successful. Korver cited a common assumption many investors face: "If you have a good team, then you can make money or eventually figure out a market." Unfortunately, this framework blends several factors together. Exaggerating and overweighting the founding team's abilities blurs how they evaluate each of the other factors in the decision-making process.

For example, an investor may partner in startups based on three categories:

- Product traction
- Founders' visions
- Market size

They assign a score out of ten total points to each category and require each category to score at least eight to move on to the next round of due diligence. Suppose the startup exceeds in the first two categories and assigns each a score of nine out of ten. However, its market size is much smaller than that of the other startups the VC usually invests in. At first, the investor assigns the market size a score of five. However, they start to think the founders are innovative enough to figure a way to make more money than the limited market size might allow them to. The investor then changes their score from a five to an eight. The startup moves on to the next round of due diligence.

In this case, the investor changed their original score of the startup's market size because they believe the founders will find a solution. This blends the two categories—founders' visions and market size—together and affects the evaluation of the market size category. They unconsciously exaggerated the founders' visions and underweighted the market size. When they evaluate the market size, they are not evaluating it based on its merit. Rather, they are evaluating it based on how they believe the founders will tackle the market size. Letting one category affect another highlights availability bias because the VC shifts the narrative away from just "market size" to "founders and the market size."

CONTEXTUALIZE STARTUP RISKS

Korver told me that reading Geoffrey Moore's book titled *Crossing the Chasm* inspired him and his co-founder, Rivera, to contextualize each risk based on the startup phases. Moore outlines three main startup stages: early-stage, crossing the chasm, and scaling.

- **Early-stage**—Develop the team, sell to early adopter customers, and related tasks when first starting companies.
- **Crossing the chasm**—Transition early adopter customers to mainstream customers and prove the startup's technology achieves business value.
- **Scaling**—Solve problems large companies face, such as setting up sales offices in different locations, dealing with cultural issues, and channeling conflict.

At each stage, Ulu Ventures assigns the probability that the startup will successfully overcome each risk. Other venture firms give absolute, general scores for each risk. Probabilities contextualize the risk management to the startup's team and stage. For example, if the Ulu team thought a startup had an 80 percent chance of overcoming a specific risk, then they would give that risk a probability of 80 percent instead of an absolute number like eight out of ten.

Using probability-weighted metrics allows Korver and Rivera to refine their risk assessment benchmarks over time. He explained, "If we have ten companies in a specific stage and each has a predicted 80 percent chance of overcoming the risks, then in ten to twelve months, eight of those ten startups should successfully overcome that risk. If only three instead of eight passed, then we can reevaluate our risk construction methodology and reflect on what we missed." This helps them observe how their predictions play out in the real world. If their prediction was considerably off from the observed results, then the team can regroup, adjust their model, and test it again in the next set of investments. This cycle creates a sustainable data-driven feedback loop of modeling, testing, and validation.

Additionally, the Ulu team can compare their probability-weighted success metrics with industry benchmarks. According to a white paper released by Cambridge Associates and Korver's own article *Picking Winners Is a Myth, but the PowerLaw Is Not,* **all the industry returns come from only 2.5 percent of investments**. If the Ulu team finds that a startup has a projected 25 percent chance of success through its probability-weighted methodology, then the startup has a ten-times probability-weighted chance of succeeding. In other words, **the Ulu team believes the startup has a ten-times greater chance of achieving success than the average startup.**

Contextualizing the chances that a startup will succeed based on the probability-weighted methodologies arms investors with a framework that is more accurate than the industry's 2.5 percent benchmark.

LAUNCH EXPERIMENTS

Korver didn't have all the answers when he and Rivera first started this data-driven approach more than a decade ago. They designed experiments, created hypotheses, captured data, and tested whether the data supported their hypotheses. If it did, then he integrated the hypothesis within his decision analysis framework. Otherwise, he launched another experiment with a different hypothesis. By iteratively developing and testing experiments, Korver identified and replaced biases with objective, data-driven explanations.

For example, earlier in his career, Korver thought founders could accurately predict the amount of dilution they would face. Early on, founders own a majority, if not all, of the equity in their companies. To bring more investors on, they must give some of their equity. Over time, the founders have much less equity than before. This process is called dilution.

After four to six years, his portfolio companies fundraised more, allowing him to compare the predicted dilution against the observed dilution. To his surprise, Korver told me, "The founders were significantly optimizing and would misestimate the dilution by two to three times." Meaning the founders gave up much more equity than they planned. Korver decided to create a new benchmark by looking at how much his portfolio companies and publicly traded companies diluted over time. He replaced the anecdote-based dilution benchmark with the new data-driven one.

Similarly, Korver measured investment returns to understand when to partner with startups. Investors can receive two types of returns—initial returns and follow-on returns. Initial returns come from the first time a VC invests, and follow-on returns originate from subsequent rounds of investments. Korver said he commonly heard that follow-on investments generate higher returns than initial investments. However, his data shows the opposite. Over time he found that, on average, initial returns generate 20 percent IRR, and the follow-on return generates about 10 percent IRR, in which IRR is the internal rate of return, or according to Investopedia, an investment's annualized rate of return and cash flow. He still has a reserve pool for follow-on investments if he wants to double down on a startup investment later, but he focuses on partnering with seed-stage companies and generating initial returns.

Tracking and comparing data points against previous hypotheses helps the Ulu team gradually form and refine a data-driven, objective, and equitable investment thesis.

KEY LESSONS TO BECOMING DATA-DRIVEN

- Identify potential sources of bias in your current methodologies.
- Ask all founders the same questions.
- When deciding whether to invest, do not let different criteria affect each other.
- Contextualize the startup's likeliness of success based on its stage and risks.
- Proactively collect data on your current operations. Refine your hypotheses by comparing your theories against the data.

CHAPTER 10

Partner with Top Co-Investors

Venture capitalists invest globally. In 2015, the World Economic Forum found the United States, Europe, China, Israel, India, and Canada most actively invest in startups. US-based VCs can adopt international strategies to build competitive advantages.

USING COMPANIES HOUSE'S DATA

The United Kingdom, unlike the United States, regulates private investments and publicizes private market data. The government agency that leads this initiative is called the Companies House. The organization monitors and administers company registrars. In the United Kingdom, according to its government website, every company that raises capital must inform the Companies House of its key financials, such as the number of shares issued and the price per share. Annually, startups must also submit their capitalization table, also known as cap table, which is a document that outlines the number of and types of shares each shareowner—founders, employees, and investors—possesses. These cap tables essentially reflect each company's valuation. The share price indicates the cost to purchase a portion of the startup. The higher the price of the share, the higher the perceived value of the company. As startups raise more capital, the share price and valuation should increase. Companies House open-sourcing this valuable insight arms UK investors with a central repository of trustworthy, consistent financial information on the private markets.

Graham Schwikkard, an alum of the Cambridge Judge Business School, one of the top business schools in the United Kingdom, set out on a journey to utilize Companies House's data to formulate a data-driven strategy and maximize VC returns. He and his early-stage venture capital firm, called the SyndicateRoom, leveraged the fact that all startups had to publicize their financial information.

In a recent conversation, Schwikkard and I discussed his investment thesis.

When referring to the cap tables and annual fundraising reports, Schwikkard explained to me that he uses the cap tables data to "piece together a lot of information about the market." His gut told him there was gold to be found. He went down a rabbit hole and hasn't looked back since.

To better understand the entrepreneurial ecosystem, SyndicateRoom extracted data on every company that raised capital and explored their progress. For example, they looked at how the share price changed over time, whether the company dissolved, and if the company achieved an acquisition or IPO. If a company raised capital several times, meaning it first raised a seed round, then a Series A, and maybe even a Series B, then the Companies House's data would show multiple changes in its share price and valuation. Schwikkard explained that a startup valuation doubling every round signals potential success. However, if a startup does not appear in the Companies House data for several years, then it may have dissolved or declared bankruptcy. Investors must use domain knowledge—information they exclusively know due to their long industry experience—to interpret trends and insights from the raw data.

Although the Companies House data is reliable, it does have its flaws. Schwikkard explained that when startups exit, they are not mandated to disclose the exit figures, such as their sale price or price per share. If they do announce such statistics, then Schwikkard can integrate them within his model. Otherwise, he must rely on the data from the startups' last valuations, which may not accurately represent the current state of the company. Sometimes, startups face hurdles that decrease their value. For example, suppose a startup sold in-person sporting event tickets and gained significant revenue and product traction in recent years. It first raised capital at a five-million-dollar valuation, then proved enough traction and strong trajectory to raise another round at a ten-million-dollar valuation two years later and was shortly afterward about to close another round at a twenty-million-dollar valuation. Unfortunately, a few months before it finalized the twenty-million-dollar valuation round, COVID-19—the infamous pandemic that shut the world down for two years—hit, and all sporting organizations suspended in-person attendance for more than a year.

The catastrophe greatly diminished ticket sales, affected the startup's potential future impact, and shrank its valuation!

Amid the uncertainty caused by the global pandemic, the startup founders decided to sell the company but did not publicize the exit's sale price. The Companies House data would only show the founders sold the startup but not the acquisition terms. If an investor saw this company's data, then they would only know the share prices and valuations from the first and second rounds, not for the upcoming third round, because it never happened, and not for the exit amount, because that information was not provided. Based on the doubled valuation between the first and second round, the investor might project the sale price to be between fifteen and twenty million dollars, when it may have been around six million dollars. Founders may sell their startups at discounts if significant risks limit the future growth.

When building his model, Schwikkard accounted for the broken data. He informed me that if a company did not announce its exit terms, then he estimated the sale price based on the startup's financial trends, previous valuations, investors' historical track records, and comparable companies' exits.

DEVELOPING A DATA-DRIVEN INVESTING THESIS
Once the SyndicateRoom team aggregated and organized each startup's data from Companies House, it examined

changes in the UK ecosystem. Schwikkard discovered two key trends, which he also published in a whitepaper on his website:

- Investors partnered with more startups every year.
- Valuations consistently increased by about 27 percent annually.

These two signs indicate that the UK venture capital market has and will continue to drastically mature. Schwikkard believes this growth can be attributed to stronger government support, such as tax breaks for startup investments.

A **consistent 27 percent annual growth** is incredibly appealing to investors, especially considering the United States' S&P 500 grows an **average of 11 percent annually**. Limited partners compare investment options with the S&P 500. If they can find a more lucrative opportunity than the S&P 500, then they may pursue it. In this case, the UK investing ecosystem may be more attractive than the S&P 500. For example, if an LP invests one hundred dollars in both the S&P 500 and the top UK startups, then within five years, the LP will achieve completely different returns.

Table 2: S&P 500 vs. UK Startup Ecosystem Returns (Assuming Constant Growth)

Year	S&P 500	UK Startup Valuations
0	$100	$100
1	$111	$127
2	$123	$161

3	$137	$205
4	$152	$260
5	$169	$330

Impressed by the UK's venture capital market, Schwikkard and his team agreed, "We wanted to find a way to take advantage of this consistent market growth as opposed to being forced to find unicorns." Companies worth more than one billion dollars are called unicorns because they are so rare to find. Schwikkard believes identifying and funding unicorns can be too variable—it's a hit or miss! Rather, he can still make money by capitalizing on the startup valuations' 27 percent growth.

Schwikkard analyzed how other VCs took advantage of the lucrative investment opportunity. He ran Monte Carlo simulations—statistical models that estimate what uncertain events will result—from the aggregated historical data.

First, he found investing once through one-time investments rather than multiple times through follow-on investments leads to higher returns. Even if the startup raises capital in the future, such as a Series A or Series B, SyndicateRoom will not invest more money. This data-driven strategy prevents SyndicateRoom from diluting its equity too much.

Second, he learned the optimal number of startups he should invest in. In the UK, according to Schwikkard, venture firms usually invest in eight to ten companies annually. But Schwikkard's statistical model found investing in **fifty startups every year** yields a "fairly narrow range of returns," making him confident he will make a set return on investments despite startups' unpredictability.

The model recommends Schwikkard invest in a new startup every week!

TRACK TOP CO-INVESTORS

Now Schwikkard just needed to figure out which startups to invest in.

He could not source deals from primarily looking at press releases. Once a startup publishes a press release on its recent round, it's too late to invest because the round has already closed. He could not look at recent Companies House data, either, because startups upload their new financial information after completing fundraising. Schwikkard eventually wondered if other investors could notify him about upcoming deals.

As previously mentioned, venture capital is currently a tight-knit, community-based profession. If Schwikkard wanted to learn about every deal, he could theoretically befriend every single investor in the country, but that's not scalable. Even if he could do that, he would still not know which ones to participate in!

Suppose one thousand startups sought to raise capital this year, but Schwikkard only wanted to invest in fifty of them. How would he prioritize which opportunities to pursue?

Once again, the SyndicateRoom team referred to Companies House. Schwikkard wrangled the cap table data to identify the investors who backed the hundred fastest growing companies. He then scraped all the deal reports to list all the startups—those that were the fastest growing and those that were not—that these top investors backed. Finally, he identified the stages at which the VCs invested in the startups. He also learned each investors' equity, each round's capital, and other metrics. Compiling this information allowed SyndicateRoom to identify, model, and replicate successful investing practices.

SyndicateRoom double-checked whether the newly discovered investing thesis works. The firm separated the startups backed by the shortlisted investors with those the investors did not back. After comparing the outcomes of each of these two groups, Schwikkard concluded that the select investors did, in fact, partner with startups that were on average more successful than the ones they didn't back. He also mapped out the other investors the top investors worked with. He created a network graph, a visualization like a spider web, that shows how often each investor works with each other and who usually works with whom in the successful deals.

Schwikkard now knew the best investors in each area. He created relationships with the top 10 percent of investors from his ranking algorithm and now invests regularly alongside them.

BEWARE OF TOO MANY COOKS IN THE KITCHEN

In exchange for access to these top deals, SyndicateRoom provides the two things these investment rounds need the most: capital and control.

First, providing immediate money is a win-win situation for both the startups and the investors. Introducing another investor who wants to give enough capital that finalizes the fundraising cycle would be a no-brainer for the startup. On the other side, these existing investors welcome Syndicate-Room because completing the fundraising process allows them to look at another startup investment.

Second, SyndicateRoom's approach means it invests in industries it doesn't have domain experience in. This might seem problematic at first because startups now seek "smart capital," where investors provide both money and strategic partnerships to help accelerate growth. Twenty years ago, there were many startups and not enough venture capital firms, so startups could not be too picky when deciding partners. Nowadays, there are many more venture capital firms, allowing startups to have more control over whom they want to partner with.

However, having too many strategic investors can hurt the startup. Schwikkard pointed out that there could be "too many cooks in the kitchen." Before SyndicateRoom enters the round, there are already people who can help the startup strategically. For example, the angel investor—or who is often the startup's first investor—is usually an expert in the startup's field. The other investors also have relevant domain experience. If an additional investor joins and offers contradictory advice, then the startup founders might get confused as to who to listen to, leading to organizational conflict. SyndicateRoom invests at a very early-stage when startups really need capital. They want to just get done with fundraising and get back to building their businesses, so they are willing to ignore lack-of-industry-relevant experience to move on. Schwikkard explained, "Investors having relevant experience comes into place when startups are looking to raise a Series A or later stage."

Schwikkard's tedious and robust research allowed SyndicateRoom to create a data-driven, scalable strategy. Schwikkard's genius was digging deep into the data to find patterns among successful venture funds and investors that others might not see. He implemented advanced statistical methods to generate a list of the top 10 percent of investors in the UK to co-invest with. He even shaped his firm's strategy to resolve the pain points of not having enough capital to complete the round. SyndicateRoom has now made almost a hundred investments to date and is gaining significant traction throughout the UK.

KEY LESSONS TO BECOMING DATA-DRIVEN

- Aggregate financial data on other VCs' successful startups to create a network map.
- Even if you cannot find other VCs' investment histories, you should identify the most successful investors and partner with them on future deals.
- Change the goal from achieving an exit to capturing the market's increasing valuations.

- Do not take a board seat so you can be flexible and attract invitations to more deals.

CHAPTER 11

Predict Startup Success

I spoke with David Coats, a Princeton University and Harvard Business School alum, who co-founded an early-stage VC firm called Correlation Ventures. He told me that when he previously invested with a different VC firm, he identified three key problems that both VCs and founders face:

1. Long fundraising timelines
2. Massive investing risk
3. Poor data

He spoke with other investors and hypothesized solutions to each of these problems, hoping to greatly improve the lives of both founders and VCs.

Long fundraising timelines—Founders spend many months fundraising. It often distracts them from building their startups. If VCs could offer rapid investment decisions that didn't invite distractions, then they may get invited to many deals.

Massive investing risk—Public market investors de-risk their portfolios by investing a small amount of capital into each opportunity. When reading a book written by John Bogle, the founder of the Vanguard Group and the creator of the public market's first index fund, Coats pondered how he could apply the same strategy in VC. He told me, "Bogle's writing got me wondering if anyone had tried a diversified index fund in venture, and no one had. That got me thinking about the portfolio construction approach toward venture." A diversified index fund mitigates extreme volatility and risks. If one investment blows up, then the others within the fund reduce the loss.

Poor data—Coats investigated whether an index fund was even possible from a data perspective. He asked other investors if they had collected venture capital financing data, assembled world-class teams, or used proven methods to look for inefficiencies and patterns in venture data. Everyone told him "no" and justified themselves with a variety of reasons why the data at that time was not good enough.

He viewed these problems as opportunities. He told me his research helped him build a "strong hypothesis that [venture capital] is an inefficient market. No one really has this financing level data, and no one uses proven methods to look for patterns. If teams spent time, money, and resources to do that, then one can find inefficiencies to take advantage of as an investor."

He co-founded Correlation Ventures, where he solves each of these opportunities by:

- Using predictive analytics to make rapid co-investment decisions in under two weeks;

- Constructing a large, diversified portfolio like a public market's index fund would have; and
- Becoming industry-leaders in data analytics.

New investors may relate to these challenges. They can learn how Coats and his team overcame them and apply the learnings for themselves.

THE JOURNEY OF INNOVATION

Coats and his co-founder, Trevor Kienzle, knew that to achieve their visions, they had to improve the underlying data. According to a 2015 Harvard Business School interview, they spent four years aggregating data themselves. The interviewee found that Coats and Kienzle "met many other VCs and entrepreneurs and negotiated nondisclosure agreements with data providers" to build a proprietary dataset with more than sixty thousand financings starting from 1987. The comprehensive and detailed dataset covered about 98 percent of all the deals during that time.

In the same interview, Coats claimed that Correlation Ventures' dataset is

"The most complete and accurate database of US-based venture capital financings in the world."

During our conversation, Coats told me that they also started a data team to build predictive analytics. In 2010, the two co-founders brought on Anu Pathria, who co-invented the Falcon Credit Card fraud detection model, an algorithm used by credit card companies to alert the cardholder about any suspicious activities. About 85 percent of credit card transactions globally use his fraud detection model. Pathria and the VC firm built the data analytics team in India to access the country's top talent.

Coats attributes Pathria as one of the main reasons why the analytics team was successful. Coats told me that Pathria possessed two strong and rare qualities: He was both an experienced data scientist and an excellent communicator. Coats exclaimed, "It is difficult to find someone who not only is a world-class data scientist but also is highly articulate and can answer technical questions and explain technical concepts in simple language." Pathria was the unicorn who had both a strong technical and business background to lead the analytics team.

The data team built the model such that founders only need to provide a handful of documents and can know within two weeks whether Correlation Ventures will invest in them or not. Each of the following steps of the investment process is founder-friendly and distraction-free:

1. **Founders provide documents**—The entrepreneur speaks with a member of the Correlation Ventures team. The founders send five pieces of readily available documents: term sheet, cap table, PowerPoint presentation, legal documents from the most recent round, and historical financials.

2. **Correlation Ventures runs a model on the founder's data**—The administrative team extracts factual data points from these documents into their proprietary model, which then outputs a score between zero and one hundred. If the score is below eighty-five, then the venture firm will rapidly and confidentially inform the entrepreneurs that they will not invest. If the startup scored an eighty-five or above, then the deal moves onto the next round.

3. **An investment board reviews the deal**—The investment team reviews the startup, the score, and the sensitivity analysis—an analytics tool that shows how certain the model is. The team also speaks with the founders and the lead VC for about thirty minutes each. If nothing unusual arises, then Correlation Ventures offers to invest in the startup.

"Founders greatly appreciate the quick turnaround time," Coats explained to me. Immediately telling the founder whether the firm will invest in their startup saves the founders precious time and resources.

Correlation Ventures' high-quality data gives them the confidence and analytics to create a portfolio like that of an index fund. Coats told me the public markets are designed to match a mark, often known as the S&P 500. The public market index funds usually invest in thirty different companies to achieve the level of diversification where returns are highly likely to equal that of the S&P 500. In VC, however, most companies fail, and some companies succeed. To achieve the same level of diversification, VCs need to invest in an average of seventy-five companies across different sectors, making the

VCs' portfolios large and highly diversified. Coats said that while typical VC firms invest in fifteen to twenty-five start-ups concentrated by sector, stage, and geography, Correlation Ventures' second fund invested in 230 startups across different sectors, stages, and categories. Coats considers the fund to be "one of most diversified venture funds in history."

Coats and Kienzle's four-year investment in building a high-quality, proprietary database gives them the luxury to help both founders and their LPs by providing investment decisions in less than two weeks and de-risking their portfolio by confidently investing across sectors.

A DETAILED EXAMINATION OF THE MODEL

Correlation Ventures can confidently invest in startups because of its robust machine learning model.

Shocked by Correlation Ventures' approach, new VCs may think that Coats's machine learning model constantly tracks hundreds—if not thousands—of factors to predict the startup success. However, that is not true. The rule of thumb in machine learning is that "less is more." The fewer impactful factors a model looks at equates to higher accuracy and predictability. If the algorithm tracks too many features, then it can overfit—the process of the algorithm finding rules to estimate predictions from the underlying training data so much that it does not perform well on new data. According to an IBM article, when the model overfits, it learns the random details of the underlying data so much that if the new data does not have the same noise, then the model cannot accurately make predictions because it cannot find the same rules to apply that it was trained on.

Coats corroborated this misconception. He explained, "[The algorithm] is not a black-box model. Rather, it capitalizes on a finite number of fundamental relationships that make sense and correlate strongly and robustly."

At a high-level, the team built the model in three steps:

1. Aggregate a preliminary list of factors to test;
2. Identify which factors individually are important to predicting startup success; and
3. Identify which factors interact well with the other factors to predict startup success.

Because both Coats and Kienzle worked in VC for a decade prior to co-founding Correlation Ventures, they knew which startup and investment characteristics they should build the model on.

Correlation Ventures originally explored many more features they thought were significant, but after testing each factor independently through univariate factor testing, they filtered and maintained the ones that were most impactful. To prove a fundamental relationship between the factor and the startup's success, the team controlled for different external variables, such as time periods, industry sectors, and stages. In other words, instead of comparing apples with oranges, they compared apples with apples and saw how the two apples were different from each other.

In general, VCs can choose many ways to do univariate analysis to know whether a variable can predict startup success. Suppose they want to use a method called statistical significance and measure the predictive ability of the company's headcount. In the example, the VC aggregates data for a hundred mid-stage, education-technology (EdTech), and Bay Area-based startups. Fifty succeeded, and fifty failed. The VC finds that most of the successful startups employed around two hundred team members, while most of the failed startups employed around fifty team members. The investors think the startup's headcount can predict startup success because the successful startups had many more employees than the failed startups did. To be more confident, they run a statistical test called the "T-test," which compares the distributions of two groups' headcount size and does, in fact, find that there was a difference. In this case, the firm's headcount can be considered statistically significant and may be kept in the model.

Going back to Correlation Ventures' methodology, passing the first round of due diligence means there is an independent significant and robust relationship between the factor and the startup's likelihood of success. It does not, however, examine how the factor interacts with the rest of the model. For example, there might be a statistically significant relationship between the number of minutes a basketball player plays in a game and the number of points they score. But if the basketball player never gets the ball—they only run up and down the court—then they would not have scored any points. Not including all relevant features can make the model vulnerable to overfitting. In this case, the omitted variable—the excluded factor that affects the rest of the model—is the number of times the player receives the ball.

The team then combined all the individually predictive factors into a multivariate model to see how all the features interact with each other. Each factor must add value to the model's predictability, meaning each must positively and tangibly impact the model's performance. Once this step is complete, the model includes only the most valuable and predictive features, all of which are found in documents the founders already have, so the founders do not have to spend more time and energy for fundraising.

This meticulous and thorough approach arms Correlation Ventures with a model that has not changed much. Coats told me every year since 2010, startups that scored highly in the model have consistently outperformed the industry prospectively. While the model's accuracy has increased over time, the number of factors has not. This speaks to the importance of tracking standard, foundational features.

COMMUNICATING THE MODEL WITH LPS

Coats's first fund was one of the first to use data analytics. He told me the group raised one of the largest debut venture funds ($165 million) during the 2008–2010 financial crisis. They then subsequently raised a $200 million second fund.

However, when raising capital from limited partners for their debut fund, they faced three main pushbacks:

- Selection model—Can Correlation Ventures make co-investment decisions using analytical models in the real world?
- Adverse selection—Is there something different about these opportunities they want access to compared to the industry average startup?
- Access—Would they be able to access these high-scoring opportunities?

SOLVING THE SELECTION MODEL AND ADVERSE SELECTION CONCERNS

The Correlations Ventures' data team applied its model on all the startups raising capital in 2017 and compared how well the predicted scores correlated with the outcomes in the future. According to Coats, this type of real-world, purely prospective examination is the most difficult test for any predictive model to pass.

There are two types of studies—retroactive and prospective. Retroactive studies examine how well the model performs on historical data. Because the outcomes of the startups are already known, users may think the model is overfitted to predict the startups in the training data accurately but may not work for future startups that the model has not seen yet. Prospective studies, however, test how well the model performs on outcomes not known at the time the model was developed. In this case, Correlation Ventures built the model on data before 2017 and then tested it on startups seeking funding in 2017. That way, the model cannot be overfitted on the 2017 data because the data did not exist when the model was created.

Correlation Ventures' model on the prospective test performed incredibly well and instilled confidence in the limited partners. After showing the model's power and accuracy, the VC firm could show the LPs why some startups performed better than others, resolving the adverse selection concern.

ACCESS TO DEALS

Once they identify potentially successful startups, Correlation Ventures approaches and persuades the startup founders to let Correlation Ventures partner with them. For example, a college basketball coach might first find the best high school basketball player in the country, but they then need to still persuade the recruit to play for them.

According to Coats, it is difficult for VCs to invest in every startup they want to. The startup might have other partnership opportunities from other VCs. To make Correlation Ventures stand out, they focus on four strategies:

1. Build an extensive network of portfolio companies and operators so startups can get the help they need;
2. Save entrepreneurs time by making fundraising with the VC incredibly easy;
3. Does not take board seats so other VCs will let them in on rounds; and
4. Have flexible funding.

The venture firm's unique value propositions have helped them invest in more than three hundred companies.

KEY LESSONS TO BECOMING DATA-DRIVEN

- Create a proprietary database across multiple years and sectors.
- Use prior investing experience to decide which factors are most important to collect.
- Invest across as many sectors, stages, and geographies as possible.
- Gather all the data → univariate test → multivariate test to find the best factors to keep.
- Run prospective tests to instill confidence in LPs.

CHAPTER 12

Measure Company Traction

One of the problems discussed in Part 1 is that early-stage startups often only have a few months' worth of financial data that may not represent future revenue. Early-stage investors can still use the principles behind data science.

When he was previously at Social Capital, Jonathan Hsu and his team developed a suite of analytics tools called the "Magic 8-Ball" to understand startup performance at a deeper level. Specifically, they can answer two questions:

- Is this startup working?
- What will happen when we add more capital?

Suppose a VC is meeting with a startup that aggregates, analyzes, and sells foot traffic data from remote cities in Asia. To generate additional traction, the startup makes some of its data free and the rest as paid. Even though the startup has little revenue to show investors, it tracks who used its data and when.

Hsu analyzes the customer data in three different ways:

- Growth accounting
- Distribution of product-market fit
- Power user curve

He open-sourced his data-driven approach on Tribe Capital's blog titled *A Quantitative Approach for Product-Market Fit* for other data-driven investors to learn from.

GROWTH ACCOUNTING

After using the product once, customers either use it again or they don't. Strong and successful products see high retention rates among customers.

Suppose the VC is doing due diligence on the foot traffic startup using Hsu's principles. They would first break down each customer into one of three types:

- **New**: Number of customers who used the product for the first time
- **Churned**: Number of customers who were previously but are not currently active, as they are no longer using the product
- **Resurrected**: Number of customers who previously churned but are now active

Strong products see an increasing number of new customers, decreasing number of churned customers, and an increasing number of resurrected customers.

According to Hsu's blog, there are three main types of revenue:

- **Expansion**: How much additional revenue a customer spent compared to before
- **Contraction**: How much lesser revenue a customer spent compared to before
- **Retained**: How much overlapping revenue a customer spent between last time and this time

Suppose a customer of the foot traffic startup actively paid money for three months. The customer spent:

- Twenty dollars in the first month
- Twenty-four dollars in the second month
- Sixteen dollars in the third month

This breaks down to:

- Second month—four dollars in expansion revenue and twenty dollars in retained revenue
- Third month—eight dollars in contracted revenue and sixteen dollars in retained revenue

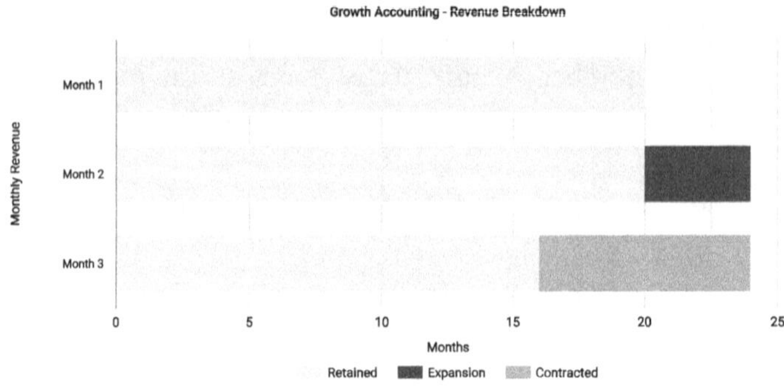

Figure 5. Customer Revenue Breakdown (Inspired by *A Quantitative Approach to Product-Market Fit*)

These numbers tell VCs that the first month of service intrigued the customer enough to sign up for a more premium service the next month. However, they were not satisfied enough to continue paying the additional amount, so they downgraded to the cheapest option in the last month before eventually becoming inactive. This leads to follow-up questions, such as:

1. Why did the customer not find enough value from the most premium data in month two?
2. Do other customers only stay active for three months?
3. Do other customers try all three products before dropping off?

DISTRIBUTION OF PRODUCT-MARKET FIT

Diving into the customer data helps new VCs find trends they might not otherwise think about.

The startup might tell the VC that, on average, customers pay ten dollars per month. Assuming they have ten customers, the startup would be earning one hundred dollars in revenue a month. In this case, ten dollars is the average contract value. Some investors might be happy with this number and move on. Others, on the other hand, may not.

Once VCs get the customer data, they can see how much each user pays. Suppose that in this example, they see that seven customers pay about seven dollars each and three customers pay seventeen dollars each. The VCs were originally told that each customer pays ten dollars on average—which is not wrong—but knowing that 50 percent of the revenue came from only three customers provides a different narrative.

Identifying how much each customer pays and seeing whether only a few make up most of the revenue helps Hsu "quantify concentration risk." In Hsu's article, he wrote that if most of the revenue comes from a handful of customers, then "the company is in some sense trending toward a consulting services company for their big customers rather than a high-margin venture-scalable product company." In other words, the VC might think that the startup has built a product that is only helpful for a few clients, which is why most of the revenue comes from them. Ideally, companies have customers who spend similar amounts of money. This de-risks the startup, because if a few users churn, then the startup can still sustain itself, thanks to the revenue from the other customers.

To visualize the potential concentration risks, data scientists can implement a "cumulative density function." Ideally, the company's sales follow the dashed line, which only happens if every customer pays an equal amount. The further away

the line of the actual sales is from the dashed line, the more
unequal—or more concentrated—the sales are.

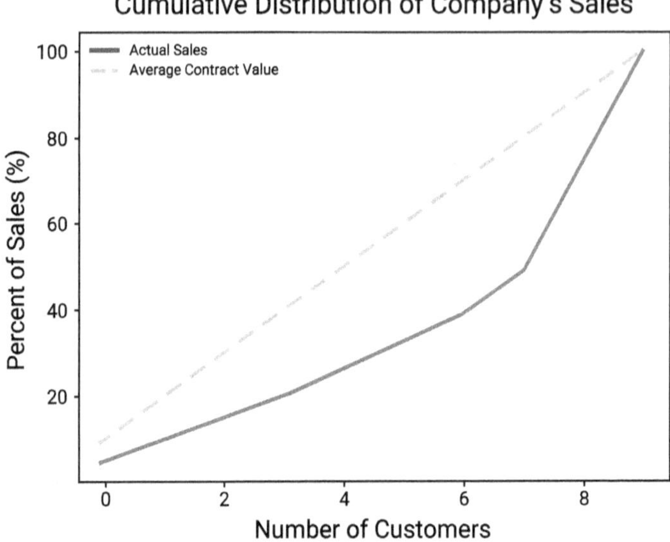

Figure 6. How Much Does Each Customer Spend? (Inspired by
A Quantitative Approach to Product-Market Fit)

The sales data can be transformed to see how much each
customer spends relative to the company's total revenue. As
each customer is added to the analysis, the percent of sales
increases. The bold line in the graph above shows that two
customers make up about 10 percent of the company's total
sales, four customers make up more than 20 percent of the
sales, six customers make up 40 percent of the sales, and
seven customers make up about 50 percent of the sales. That
means the seven least-paying customers account for 50 percent of the company's revenue, and three customers make
up the remaining 50 percent. Because the company earned

one hundred dollars and the **smallest seven customers** pay about fifty dollars, they pay an average of **about seven dollars each**. The **three largest customers pay** a combined total of fifty dollars, so they pay an average of **about seventeen dollars each**.

After looking at this graph, VCs can:

- Explore ways to encourage the customers who pay seven dollars to start paying closer to seventeen dollars; and
- Strategize ways to prevent the large-paying customers from churning. The startup can't afford to lose them.

POWER USER CURVE

Hsu uses many of his data analysis skills from his time at Facebook to measure company performance too. Two of the most legendary investors are Li Jin and Andrew Chen. They both work with the highly respected Andreessen Horowitz venture capital firm. Chen wrote a blog post titled *The Power User Curve: The Best Way to Understand Your Most Engaged Users*, where he described how the Growth Team at Facebook measured user activity. They coined the term "L30," also known as the "Power User Curve," which is a graph that visualizes how distributed user engagement is over time.

The illustration below shows the Power User Curve for a company that has high recurring engagement. Many users only engage with the product for a few days, while others use it almost every day. A high concentration of daily active users signals a strong product-market fit. This helps venture capitalists understand the user engagement more clearly than a statement like, "On average, users interact with us for thirteen days every month." Identifying a loyal group of customers motivates investors to think of additional ways to create similar high-value features for users.

According to Chen's blog, Jin and Chen believe that "great companies with great Power User Curves have a smile."

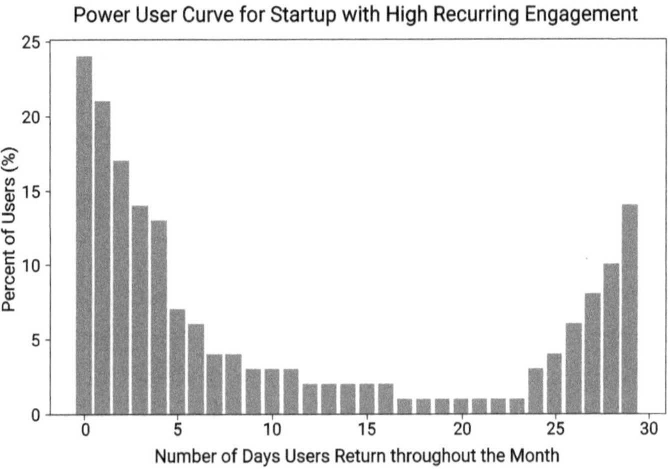

Figure 7. Power User Curve for High Engagement (Inspired by Andrew Chen's Blog)

Unfortunately, not every company shows a strong daily engagement rate. If customers do not frequently utilize the product, then the company will show a low recurring engagement rate. In the chart below, no customers use the product more than fifteen times in the month. This can be a huge red flag to an investor. The startup could have told the investors something like, "On average, our customers use the product once every week." This may sound appealing at first, but once investors see the Power User Curve below, they may conclude that customers do not find enough value to engage with the product repeatedly.

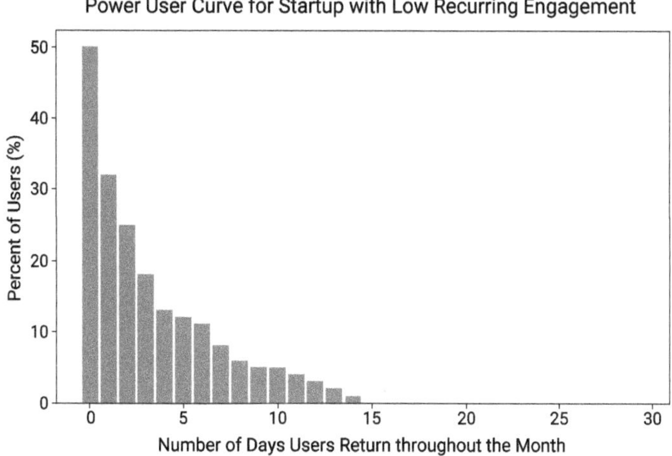

Figure 8. Power User Curve for Low Engagement (Inspired by Andrew Chen's Blog)

KEY LESSONS TO BECOMING DATA-DRIVEN
- Analyze the data to look for distributions and not just static numbers.
- Looking at how concentrated a startup's customer base is helps find red flags.
- Break the revenue down to see whether the startup is gaining or losing customers.

CHAPTER 13

Build Tools with Email Data

———

You send emails.

I send emails.

We all send emails.

Emails dominate communication. The online statistics database Statistica estimates that in 2019, people sent and received 293.6 billion emails daily!

Imagine using at least **some** of that data to build VC data tools. The industry would no longer face the problem of data sparsity.

Yasyf Mohamedali did that!

VCWIZ HELPED FOUNDERS AND INVESTORS

Mohamedali, who received his bachelor's and master's degrees from the Massachusetts Institute of Technology (MIT), set out on a mission to leverage raw email data to help founders fundraise quicker and VCs invest using more data-driven strategies.

For his master's thesis, the 2018 *Forbes* 30 Under 30 winner built VCWiz, a tool to help first-time founders find and connect with seed investors. First Round Capital, an early-stage venture firm that invested in top companies such as Uber, GOAT, and Blue Apron, sponsored Mohamedali's work. He explained his project in his thesis titled *Matching Startup Founders to Investors: A Tool and a Study.*

When I spoke with Mohamedali, he said he searched for high-volume datasets that provided more information than public ready-made datasets did so he could build the most accurate and useful tool he could. Specifically, he wanted to gather "network data between founders and founders and founders and investors. The only way to get that was from email!" Aggregating email data allowed him to perform higher-quality analysis, such as sentiment analysis, which lets him see how positive or negative a founder is based on the words they wrote in their email, whom they communicate with the most, and other high-impact statistics. For example, he could measure the quality of a relationship based on how two people communicated over email. He informed me, "The difference between sending a really formal email and casual messages back and forth tells you so much about a relationship." That level of analysis is hard to replicate using solely public data.

To build his email dataset, he asked users from VCWiz, his founder-investor matching tool, whether they were willing to share access to their emails for research purposes.

Thousands agreed.

After months of research and development, Mohamedali launched his product and found ways both founders and investors could benefit from email-based data tools.

VCWIZ GENUINELY HELPED FOUNDERS

First-time founders loved his product, as it helped them discover VCs they can partner with that they may not have learned about otherwise. As described in Mohamedali's paper, a user exclaimed that thanks to VCWiz, "We discovered several relevant investors that weren't on our radar, and we ended up building a robust target investor list that expedited our process."

By the time Mohamedali published his thesis, 250 founders actively used his product monthly, and 1,200 founders used it at least once. Registered users visited an average of four investor profiles monthly. The founders who allowed VCWiz to track their emails shared thirty-three emails with investors monthly too! Users highly appreciated the investors and firms' research pages, as that is where most of the users spent their time on the product.

Mohamedali's paper also identified the most important investor-related information founders seek when fundraising:

- Recent press releases on the VC firm
- Co-investors the VC frequently works with
- Prior investment history
- Biography of each VC partner
- Topics VC partners write about in blogs and social media

VCWiz helped bridge the fundraising gap for first-time founders by providing the contacts and research they previously lacked.

PREDICTING A FOUNDER'S FUNDRAISING SUCCESS

Emails represent networks.

Person A sending Person B an email establishes a connection. Person B responding to Person A modifies the one-way connection into a two-way relationship because Person B cared enough about Person A to respond. Every time they reply to each other, their relationship strengthens. If Person A introduces Person B to Person C, then Person B must be valuable enough for Person C to meet. Quantifying similar relationships from the email data lays the foundations for Mohamedali's model.

According to Mohamedali's paper, the MIT graduate student possessed emails from more than 400,000 individuals and identified email relationships between more than 7,500 founders and 2,100 investors. He saw how frequently investors and founders emailed each other and who they introduced each other to. He leveraged the large dataset to build a model that he called "FounderRank" to predict the probability that a founder would successfully fundraise their round.

He identified three characteristics that only network data may show:

1. **Importance**—How central is the founder in their own network? If other people introduced them to other founders or investors, then they must be well-known. Important founders are viewed as experts in their fields, and as a result, investors may find them to be less risky to partner with.
2. **Influence**—How helpful is the founder to other founders? If the founder has a strong influence, then they can make many future introductions.
3. **Access**—How close is an investor with the founder? If the founder had access to multiple investors and chose to speak to one investor, then that investor must be special.

His model found **the most important feature that signals whether a founder will raise capital is their access to investors.** Specifically, he wrote, "Founders who have a short average distance to investors tend to see success fundraising." Without this model, VCs cannot easily measure how likely a founder will fundraise. In his paper, Mohamedali wrote that in the status quo, many firms "haphazardly [pick] new companies to investigate based on 'gut feelings.'" He even found that one investor chooses which startups to respond to based on the alphabetical order of inbound requests! Investors can leverage this data-driven model to accurately predict whether a startup will complete its fundraising or not, so they know who they should talk to.

INVESTORS CAN STOP MISSING OUT ON DEALS

Such data-driven email tools can help investors prioritize which deals to look at.

In my call with Mohamedali, he told me VC analysts get hundreds of inbound emails from founders every year. They go through most emails, review the pitch, and respond to the founder if they think the startup is a good fit.

Responding to each email can take a long time. By the time a VC analyst reviews an inbound request, the startup might have already closed their round, making it too late to invest even if the VC wanted to. Mohamedali believes venture firms can use their historical email data as a training data set and build a tool that measures the likelihood that a startup will raise a round soon based on the email text.

These data products would not automate VC jobs. It would only help supplement their current operations. During our call, Mohamedali exclaimed, "Just because an email is marked as a priority with this tool doesn't mean you should back them. Don't use it to make investment decisions. Rather, use it to prioritize who you talk to." Ranking which founders to speak to can accelerate deals being signed and reduce the number of lost investment opportunities. Additionally, they can identify and help first-time founders who may not have many VC connections, thus making VC more equitable. Network data can solve many problems VCs currently face.

EMAIL DATA IS BEST SUITED FOR EARLY-STAGE STARTUPS

Tracking and measuring email conversations can be a powerful tool for early-stage investors. Later-stage startups, however, may be too mature to extract insights for. During our conversation, Mohamedali broke down two reasons why he thinks later-stage investors may find less value from email data.

First, founders' emails can suggest which new investors the founders should speak to. Early-stage founders reach out to many investors they often don't already know to maximize their chances of receiving funding. As a startup reaches its later stages, founders themselves don't spend as much time finding new investors as before. Rather, according to Mohamedali, by then, founders already know who they want to raise from, and current investors act on behalf of the founders to discover any new investors.

Second, once founders find their investors, they often communicate less over email and more through text messages, in-person meetups, or other personal interactions. As a result, later-stage companies have less investor-focused email data to extract than before.

Mohamedali's research helped break down the systematic barriers that first-time founders face. His tool can both help founders fundraise quicker and assist investors in prioritizing the order of the companies they look at based on their investment thesis.

KEY LESSONS TO BECOMING DATA-DRIVEN

- The VC's emails can be an untouched gold mine of data to analyze.
- Founders with the most access to investors have the highest chance of fundraising success. Building tools like VCWiz can help match first-time founders with investors.
- Investors can predict which startups are most likely to finish fundraising the soonest so they can prioritize the order of startups they speak to accordingly.
- Email data works best for early-stage startups.

CHAPTER 14

Arm Retail Investors with Data

As I delved deeper into my research, I became more and more excited about investing in startups. Investors can leverage data in multiple ways to invest with more confidence and clarity.

I only faced one problem, though.

I'm not currently an accredited investor. I can't invest in the startups that I researched.

According to Investopedia, the Securities and Exchange Commission (SEC) defines an accredited investor as one who either has:

- Net worth of one million dollars or more, where they cannot include their primary residence as part of their net worth; or

- Annual gross income of $200,000 or more for two con-
  secutive years for individuals or $300,000 or more for two
  consecutive years for married couples.

These stringent financial requirements limit the number of people who can invest in the private capital markets. In 2020, the financial company named Don't Quit Your Day Job reported that "roughly 10.6 percent of all American households were accredited in 2020."

Only 10 percent of American households can technically invest in the private markets as accredited investors!

The SEC is aware of these limitations. In fact, in August 2020, the SEC amended and loosened its requirements. According to its press release, the following are some groups who can now invest in the private markets:

- Individuals who are "knowledgeable employees" of the fund;
- Limited liability companies with at least five million dollars in assets; and
- Family offices with five million dollars or more in assets
  under management (AUM).

Despite these changes, I still wouldn't be able to invest in the private markets.

That's what I thought until I heard about regulation crowdfunding.

Regulation crowdfunding allows non-accredited investors to pool their money together and partner with startups that are raising capital from the public. Main Street—non-institutional investors—can invest in certain startups and receive startup equity in return, making investing more equitable.

This made me excited. I was ecstatic!

However, venture capital firms still have the capital and labor resources to spend the time, energy, and money that retail investors might not have. For example, when a venture firm is interested in a company, they often call the startup's customers, speak with the founding team multiple times, and get access to internal, financial, and operational data. On the contrary, since retail investors are too strapped by their daily jobs, chores, and responsibilities, they have limited time and money to invest in buying data and developing tools to help them make wise investment decisions. They need efficient and readily available analytics to invest confidently.

TAKATKAH AND KINGSCROWD TOOLKIT

KingsCrowd built data analytics tools to aggregate, analyze, and rate startups raising capital through regulation crowdfunding. Serving as the first independent ratings and analytics platform for the online private markets, KingsCrowd analyzed thousands of preseed to pre-IPO opportunities from more than fifty online private marketplaces. This arms Main Street investors with the actionable insights and research they need to make the best investment decision they can.

KingsCrowd wasn't always as data-driven as they currently are.

Ahmad Takatkah changed the data scene.

Before Takatkah joined the fintech data company, KingsCrowd only analyzed startups manually and qualitatively. During our conversation, Takatkah told me the firm's rating system was very opinion-based. For example, the KingsCrowd team would look at the materials that the startup submits, such as their pricing, founders' background, and pitch deck, and, as Takatkah described, "sit down to see if the startup is a top deal, a deal to watch, or one to pass on. They had a subjective rating, but they wanted to get an objective rating." Although the manual approach allowed them to be detailed, it took too long and was not scalable. Takatkah was hired to analyze and rank startups based on data rather than opinions.

Takatkah is no stranger to venture capital or data.

When Takatkah lived in Jordan—his homeland—he worked in two venture firms and a startup. When in VC, he found that many companies he genuinely thought would succeed ended up failing. Frustrated yet determined, Takatkah made it his mission to find new ways to invest more successfully within the Middle East. When actively exploring new venture capital models, he often traveled to the United States—specifically Silicon Valley. He told me that speaking with experienced investors let him "learn from their experience and avoid reinventing the wheel." Specifically, he noticed the top investors tracked data on the startups they were interested in working with—a habit not as common back home.

Inspired by how great of an investor he could be with his new learnings, he moved to the United States in 2016. Takatkah joined Carta, a technology startup that manages cap tables for venture capital firms and startups. Carta has access to unparalleled amounts of data across the entrepreneurship world. In 2019, 700,000 shareholders, 11,000 companies, and 143 venture firms used Carta, making it one of the most popular software in the venture industry. In 2021, the data firm was valued at more than seven billion dollars. At Carta, Takatkah spent years working with large volumes of anonymized private market data. He aggregated and analyzed market trends, stock options, compensation, and fund performance and developed a strong, data-driven understanding of the private markets—a rare skill to have.

When Takatkah began working at KingsCrowd, he essentially started from ground zero. To truly empower unaccredited investors and support startups, he had to transform the company's culture, compile and aggregate fresh data, and deliver actionable insights for users who are new to investing.

That's quite a challenge!

He broke his approach down into three steps:

- **Data collection**—What metrics should he track to help Main Street investors decide whether to invest?

- **Data analysis**—What does the data show?
- **Data visualization**—How does he display the information so unaccredited investors know what it means?

Data scientists who want to break into venture capital can follow KingsCrowd's approach and build their own side projects to showcase their abilities to collect data from scratch and create actionable tools for investors to use.

KINGSCROWD DATA COLLECTION

When Takatkah first started collecting data, he expected to gather very few data points. After all, traditional venture capital firms only invest in the private markets, so they only have access to internal, private data on the startups they are already talking to, not new ones who they have yet to meet. Regulatory crowdfunding, however, mandates its startups to publicly disclose key information, such as their finances and future plans.

This solved one of the biggest problems that private markets face: limited data.

Energized and determined to capture as much data as possible, Takatkah built a team to manually extract more than 130 data points for each startup. He created these data points from online sources and the materials that the startups featured themselves. For example, he collected data from the Securities and Exchange Commission (SEC). Takatkah told me, "Any organization that raised capital from the public has to file with the SEC, meaning the startups' financial data is publicly available." He collected data on their current investors, product reviews, attainable market, competitors, and founder background from online platforms such as LinkedIn and other crowdfunding platforms like Republic. Additionally, he used data from the companies' profiles. He explained that "whenever a company wants to raise from the crowd, they list a lot of data and information about themselves and reasons why [the crowd] should invest with [them]." This meant Takatkah could gather and use information from the pitch deck, videos, business models, and sales.

Takatkah finally collected enough of the right data that represented the startup in every possible way to build a strong, robust analytics model.

KINGSCROWD DATA ANALYSIS

Once Takatkah had the data he needed, he needed to somehow compare each startup with each other.

Why should one startup be ranked higher than another?

What makes one startup "better" than the other?

Why should a user invest in one startup and not the others?

To answer these questions, Takatkah back-tested the historical data. He looked at all the startups that raised capital through regulation crowdfunding. By comparing the companies that did meet their fundraising goals against those that didn't, he fully understood the startup investing landscape. He had both the access to data for both successful and unsuccessful companies and the visibility on what prevented startups from not reaching their fundraising goals. That solves venture capital's problem of asymmetric data!

Although this might sound counterintuitive, Takatkah didn't completely rely on the data. Great data scientists leverage both their data-savvy skills and industry experience to create models that tell a data-driven and understandable story.

To balance his data-driven model with industry knowledge, Takatkah and KingsCrowds created two sets of scores: one quantifiable score from his model and one qualitative score that the firm already had. Takatkah would only recommend a startup if both the quantitative and qualitative scores summed up was greater than a benchmark. For example, if the investment committee assigned a high qualitative score but the algorithm gave a low quantitative score, then Takatkah would not score the startup highly. They believed that startups with both high qualitative scores and high quantitative scores have the best chances to successfully raise capital or be acquired in the future.

Relying on both industry experience from the investment committee and data-driven predictions from the model makes KingsCrowd's recommendations trustworthy.

KINGSCROWD DATA VISUALIZATION

Takatkah's final step was to display the startups' calculated ratings to KingsCrowd customers. A model's accuracy or insight only matters if users understand the data.

After iterations of product testing, he learned that users want to know both the overall score and the factors used to build that score. Many machine learning teams face this challenge. For example, SeatGeek, a search engine for sports, music, and other live events, developed an algorithm that determines whether a ticket price is too expensive or a fair price. To educate its customers about its models, SeatGeek wrote articles about how it developed the algorithm. In 2015, it wrote an article with Harvard Business School that articulated that its price prediction model is based on the seat quality, historical ticket prices, comparable ticket prices, and the event host's popularity. Open-sourcing and explaining their methodologies to their customers helps data-driven organizations increase retention and brand trustworthiness. Takatkah chose to publish the scores, factors, and visualizations, such as line graphs and bar charts, to show how much money the startup has raised and the calculated scores per factor. Customers can use this information to understand whether they should invest in a startup.

Takatkah's approach is remarkable because he used publicly available data to build data-driven startup recommendations for new investors. Both you and I have access to that same data!

KEY LESSONS TO BECOMING DATA-DRIVEN

- Startups seeking to raise capital through regulatory financing have more accessible data than traditional startups do.

- Hire a team to collect data quickly and accurately. Create training guides that explain how you want the data to be collected.
- Do not completely automate your scoring. Include a human-created, qualitative score to supplement your model's quantitative score.
- Explain how you created your predictive models to your end user.

CHAPTER 15

The Ultimate Data-Driven Investor

At the beginning of the book, we defined a data-driven investor as someone who:

- Runs experiments to test hypotheses;
- Makes objective decisions based on data;
- Actively collects proprietary and public data; and
- Builds data products to solve problems.

Our journey of becoming a data-driven investor first started with understanding the biggest current problems in venture capital, then outlining the steps required to become data-driven, and finally exploring several data-driven techniques that solve our biggest problems. An ultimate data-driven investor actively embodies each of the four pillars.

RUNNING EXPERIMENTS TO TEST HYPOTHESES.

Like how Ulu Venture's Korver first hypothesized equity dilution over time, data-driven investors can create theories, track data over time, and determine whether their initial assumptions were correct or not. If they were incorrect, then a data-driven investor would modify the theory and rerun the experiment.

MAKES OBJECTIVE DECISIONS BASED ON DATA.

Like how Jonathan Hsu measures startup engagement objectively, data-driven investors listen to what the data says. They may establish frameworks or modify their data pipelines to remove biases from the data.

ACTIVELY COLLECTS PROPRIETARY AND PUBLIC DATA.

Like how David Coats invested resources to build his own proprietary dataset, data-driven investors must identify, collect, and clean internal and external data. They know that public data may be inconsistent, so they consistently track their own internal data and make immediate business value.

BUILDS DATA PRODUCTS TO SOLVE PROBLEMS.

Like how Ahmad Takatkah built analytics tools to help retail investors know which startups to partner with, data-driven investors leverage business analytics or machine learning techniques to make their data actionable. They develop data products that help find competitive insights that are difficult for non-data-driven investors to easily find.

Venture capital has been and always will be a human-centric industry. However, the next wave of successful investors may leverage data technologies to spot trends and insights that others may not quickly identify. As an industry, we are **very early** in the data-driven journey.

The best time to start becoming data-driven was yesterday.

The second best time is now!

Acknowledgments

Thank you to everyone who supported me in writing this book.

To New Degree Press, thank you for showing the light and helping me publish my first book. To my editor, Ryan Porter, thank you for believing in me and guiding me throughout this process. To New Degree Press founder Eric Koester, thank you for creating an amazing program to help first-time authors publish. To Amanda Brown and the proofreading team, thank you for your meticulousness and patience. To everyone else at New Degree Press who contributed in any big or small way, thank you for all your hard work. To my beta readers, thank you for investing your time and money in this journey. I will always remember your trust in me.

A special shoutout to my family, especially my mother—thank you for all your support.

Ever since I was five years old, I have dreamed of publishing a book. You all helped turn that dream into a reality.

Special thank you to my interviewees for taking the time to speak with me:

Ahmad Takatkah, Beiming Liu, Clint Korver, David Coats, Graham Schwikkard, Henry Apfel, Jonathan Hsu, Julian Rachman, Steven Kaplan, Tim Harsch, Will Bricker, and Yasyf Mohamedali

Special thanks to my interviewees who also preordered my book:

Clint Korver, David Coats, Graham Schwikkard, Julian Rachman, Tim Harsch

Special thanks to my early supporters:

Abhinav Kejriwal, Alan Liang, Andrei Caprau, Andrew Borchert, Anjoo & Phool Chand Bhatnagar, Anju & Naresh Mathur, Anoop Gundala, Anupma Seth, Apaar Bhatnagar, Arun Shekar, Arya Vajpayee, Ashby Foltz, Avantika Bhatnagar, Bill Zhang, Bimal M Patel, Bryan Bischof, Calon Lochridge, Carlyn Chinen, Charlie McMurry, Devesh Dalmia, Dhaivat Pandya, DonJe Lee, Eric Koester, Faeez Juneja, Harsh Bhatnagar, Heather Vo, Jacob Goena, Justin Wang, Keegan Simzer, Kshitij Seth, Madan Nakka, Madhuri Lata Srivastava, Maki Imano, Mandalynne Goena, Mangalam Manishankar, Manju & Shyam Tiwari, Manohar Hiremagalore, Manoj Bhatnagar, Marco Morales, Mayank Bhatnagar, Meghana Vadranam, Mukul Bhatnagar, Munira Pirani, Neeraj Alavala, , Neetha Kotagiri, Niraj Mathur, Nishith Oza, Puneet Bhatnagar, Punita Bhatnagar, Rita Sharma, Robin Ghosh, Rudra Sharma , Sandeep Verma, Sanjay Johar, Saran Bhatnagar,

Saroj Bhatnagar, Saurav Mittal, Sheel Chandra, Shital Mathur, Shubhi Asthana, Shyamala Acharya, Sohum Shah, Sridhar Munagala, Suvashis Nandy, Soami Saran Bhatnagar, Tarun Bakhru, Vagish Sinha, Vidhur Kumar, Vijay Gaur, Vincent Zhu, Vivek Datta, and Yanay Rosen

APPENDIX

CHAPTER 1

Fernando, Jason. Investopedia. "What Is an Initial Public Offering (IPO)?" Accessed September 12, 2021. https://www.investopedia.com/terms/i/ipo.asp

Gravagna, Nicole, and Pater Adams. Venture Capital For Dummies. Hoboken: Wiley, 2013.

Hayes, Adam. Investopedia. "Exit Strategy." Accessed August 11, 2021. https://www.investopedia.com/terms/e/exitstrategy.asp

Kenton, Will. Investopedia. "Limited Partner." Accessed September 12, 2021. https://www.investopedia.com/terms/l/limited-partner.asp

Maverick, J.B. Investopedia. "What Is the Average Annual Return for the S&P 500?" Accessed August 14, 2021. https://www.investopedia.com/ask/answers/042415/what-average-annual-return-sp-500.asp.

CHAPTER 2

Abdullah, Sammy. Crunchbase. "How Long Does It Take a Startup to Exit?" Accessed September 19, 2021. https://about.crunchbase.com/blog/startup-exit/.

August Capital. "Portfolio." Accessed December 12, 2020. https://www.augustcap.com/portfolio/.

Barnes, Ryan. Investopedia. "Due Diligence in 10 Easy Steps." Accessed October 20, 2021. https://www.investopedia.com/articles/stocks/08/due-diligence.asp

Columbia Business School. "How to Make an Analytics Startup Successful." May 4, 2016. Video, 1:26:54. https://www.youtube.com/watch?v=rZPrOwzoC9Q&t=823s.

Stebbings, Harry. "Manu Kumar on how venture capitalists manage their time." TechCrunch. May 23, 2016, 4:30 a.m. PDT https://techcrunch.com/2016/05/23/manu-kumar-on-how-venture-capitalists-manage-their-time/.

Tardi, Carla. Investopedia. "What Is a Portfolio?" Accessed October 20, 2021. https://www.investopedia.com/terms/p/portfolio.asp

Walk, Hunter. "How VCs Spend Their Time. Err, How This VC Spends His Time." Hunter Walk: 99% Humble, 1% Brag (blog). January 5, 2014. https://hunterwalk.com/2014/01/05/how-vcs-spend-their-time-err-how-this-vc-spends-his-time/.

CHAPTER 3

Chen, James. Investopedia. "Survivorship Bias." Accessed September 20, 2021. https://www.investopedia.com/terms/s/survivorshipbias.asp.

Dean, Tomer. "The Meeting That Showed Me the Truth About VCs." TechCrunch. June 1, 2017. https://techcrunch.com/2017/06/01/the-meeting-that-showed-me-the-truth-about-vcs/.

Elzinga, Didier. "The Impact of an Exit on Culture, According to Data." *Culture Amp Blog,* Culture Amp (blog). 2017. https://www.cultureamp.com/blog/the-impact-of-an-exit-on-culture-according-to-data.

FundComb. "The Oldest Venture Capital Funds." Accessed October 18, 2021. https://fundcomb.com/lists/oldest/venture-capital.

G. C. Calafiore, M. Hillary Morales, V. Tiozzo and S. Marquie, "A Classifiers Voting Model for Exit Prediction of Privately Held Companies," 2020 European Control Conference (ECC), 2020, pp. 615–620, doi: 10.23919/ECC51009.2020.9143833.

Kaplan, Steven N and Lerner, Josh. "Venture Capital Data: Opportunities and Challenges." National Bureau of Economic Research, 22500 (2016): 1–18. http://www.nber.org/papers/w22500.

Potter, Sara B. "US IPO Market: SPACS Drive 2020 IPOs to a New Record." FactSet. January 7, 2021. https://insight.factset.com/u.s.-ipo-market-spacs-drive-2020-ipos-to-a-new-record.

US Securities and Exchange Commission. *Investor Bulletin: Investing in an IPO*. Washington DC.

CHAPTER 4

Alejandro, Cremades. "How Long It Takes To Raise Capital For A Startup." Forbes. Jan 3, 2019. https://www.forbes.com/sites/alejandrocremades/2019/01/03/how-long-it-takes-to-raise-capital-for-a-startup/?sh=20918fde7a41.

CB Insights. *Venture Capital Funding Report Q4 2020*. New York. 2021.

Harris, Aaron and Tam, Janelle. "Investor Funnels for Series As." YCombinator (blog). May 29, 2019. https://blog.ycombinator.com/investor-funnels-for-series-as/.

Johnson, Del. "Ban Warm Introductions!" *Medium*. August 6, 2019. https://medium.com/@DelJohnsonVC/ban-warm-introductions-1e69169d57ba.

Kapor Capital. *2019 Kapor Capital Impact Report*. 2019. Oakland: 2019.

Kerby, Richard. "Where Did You Go to School?" *Medium*. July 30, 2018. https://medium.com/@kerby/where-did-you-go-to-school-bde54d846188.

Panoramic Ventures. *The State of Startups in the Southeast 2021*. Atlanta: 2021.

Shieber, Jonathan. "A Focus On Diversity Reaps Rewards for This Los Angeles Investor." *TechCrunch*. April 12, 2019. https://techcrunch.com/2019/04/12/a-focus-on-diversity-reaps-rewards-for-this-los-angeles-investor/.

CHAPTER 6

Bricker, Will. *Venture Systemization*. New York. 2021.

Tim Brady. YCombinator. "Building Culture." Accessed May 19, 2021. https://www.ycombinator.com/library/6r-building-culture

CHAPTER 7

Aase, Geir. "Meltwater Acquires Business Information Company Owler for $24.5 Million in a Combination of Cash and Equity."

Backlink.io. *Reddit User and Growth Stats (Updated Oct 2021)*. Backlink, 2021.

Crunchbase. "Search Companies." Accessed July 16, 2021. https://www.crunchbase.com/discover/organization.companies.

GlobeNewswire, June 18, 2021. Meltwater. website. https://www.globenewswire.com/news-release/2021/06/18/2249608/0/en/Meltwater-acquires-business-information-company-Owler-for-24-5-million-in-a-combination-of-cash-and-equity.html, accessed August 23, 2021.

Hargrave, Marshall. Investopedia. "Crowdsourcing." Accessed September 24, 2021. https://www.investopedia.com/terms/c/crowdsourcing.asp.

Miller, Rebecca. "How Does Crunchbase Get My Information?" *Crunchbase*. 2018.. https://support.crunchbase.com/hc/en-us/articles/360001360088-How-does-Crunchbase-get-my-information-.

CHAPTER 9

Cambridge Associates. *Venture Capital Disrupts Itself: Breaking the Concentration Curse*. November 2015.

Korver, Clint. "Picking Winners is a Myth, but the PowerLaw is Not" *Medium*. May 29, 2018. https://medium.com/ulu-ventures/successful-vcs-need-at-least-one-outlier-to-have-a-well-performing-fund-c122c799dfb3.

CHAPTER 10

Cambridge Associates. *Venture Capital Disrupts Itself: Breaking the Concentration Curse*. November 2015.

Companies House. GOV.UK. Your Personal Information on the Companies House Register." Accessed April 1, 2021. https://www.gov.uk/guidance/your-personal-information-on-the-public-record-at-companies-house

Schwikkard, Graham. *A Data-Driven Approach to Venture Fund Portfolio Building*. London: SyndicateRoom 2020.

Vanham, Peter. "Which Countries Have the Most Venture Capital Investments?" *World Economic Forum.* July 28, 2015. https://www.weforum.org/agenda/2015/07/which-countries-have-the-most-venture-capital-investments/.

CHAPTER 11

Storrs, Francis. "Data-Driven Diligence." *Harvard Business School Alumni.* September 1, 2015. https://www.alumni.hbs.edu/stories/Pages/story-bulletin.aspx?num=4835.

CHAPTER 12

Chen, Andrew. "The Power User Curve: The Best Way to Understand Your Most Engaged Users." Andrew Chen (blog). https://andrewchen.com/power-user-curve/.

Hsu, Jonathan. "A Quantitative Approach to Product Market Fit." Tribe Capital (blog). July 14, 2019. https://tribecap.co/a-quantitative-approach-to-product-market-fit/.

CHAPTER 13

Mohamedali, Yasyf. "Matching Startup Founders to Investors: A Tool and a Study." DSpace@MIT (2018):1–152. https://dspace.mit.edu/handle/1721.1/119731.

Statistica. "Number of Sent and Received E-mails per Day Worldwide from 2017 to 2025." Accessed October 11, 2021. https://www.statista.com/statistics/456500/daily-number-of-e-mails-worldwide/.

CHAPTER 14

Don't Quit Your Day Job. "How Many Accredited Investors Are There in America?" Don't Quit Your Day Job. June 8, 2021. https://dqydj.com/accredited-investors-in-america/.

Harvard Business School. "SeatGeek—Creating Price Transparency in the Ticket Market." Harvard Business School. November 22, 2015. https://digital.hbs.edu/platform-digit/submission/seatgeek-creating-price-transparency-in-the-ticket-market/.

Hayes, Adam. Investopedia. "Accredited Investor." Accessed September 29, 2021. https://www.investopedia.com/terms/c/crowdsourcing.asp.

Loizos, Connie. "Carta Was Just Valued at $1.7 Billion by Andreessen Horowitz, in a Deal Some See as Rich." *TechCrunch*. May 6, 2019. https://techcrunch.com/2019/05/06/carta-was-just-valued-at-1-7-billion-by-andreessen-horowitz-in-a-deal-some-see-as-rich/.

Loizos, Connie. "Carta Says It Just Used Its Own Product to Establish a New—and Far Higher—Valuation for Itself." TechCrunch. August 13, 2021. https://techcrunch.com/2021/08/13/carta-says-it-just-used-its-own-product-to-establish-a-new-and-far-higher-valuation-for-itself/.

US Security and Exchange Commission. "SEC Modernizes the Accredited Investor Definition." Press release, February 13, 2018. Website. https://www.sec.gov/news/press-release/2020-191, accessed October 12, 2021.